Reggie Lewis

Quiet Grace

Reggie Lewis

Quiet Grace

Craig Windham

ACTEX Publications
Winsted, Connecticut

Manufactured in the United States of America

10 9 8 7 6 5 4 3 2 1

Cover Design and Interior Artwork by
    T-Square Advertising and Design

Library of Congress Cataloging-in-Publication Data

Windham, R. Craig, date.
    Reggie Lewis : quiet grace / R. Craig Windham.
        p.   cm.
    Includes bibliographical references and index.
    ISBN 1-56698-164-6
    1. Lewis, Reggie, 1965-1993.   2. Basketball players--
United States--Biography.   I. Title.
    GV884.L48W55   1995
    796.323'092--dc20   95-10448
    [B]   CIP

ISBN: 1-56698-164-6

Contents

Acknowledgements

In the weeks following Reggie Lewis' passing, it seemed that his memory would forever be obscured by the news media focus on the "tragic" aspects of his death. The idea for this book originated with my friend Dick London, who heads ACTEX Publications in Winsted, Connecticut. He had a simple vision: to cut through the cloud of controversy, and tell the empowering story of this wonderful young man who went from the playgrounds of Baltimore to NBA stardom. I am most grateful to Dick for inviting me to help make that vision a reality.

At each step in Reggie's life there were relatives and close friends who played key roles in helping him along his path. One of my greatest joys in writing this book was the opportunity to involve many of my own close friends and family members, who gave me the gift of their love and support. Most notable among them was Lillian Ruffin. She was along for the entire journey, constantly offering me assistance and encouragement, especially when unanticipated obstacles and frictions threatened to derail the project. Tim Groves, a close friend since we were choirboys together at the Washington National Cathedral, did a superb job of editing the manuscript and giving me valuable feedback.

The spirit of the book was captured beautifully by Lisa Thorén in her cover design. I also received helpful input and inspiration from Frank and Linda Peters; Stu Rushfield; my parents; my brother, Cris; my nephew, Bryan; Guy Kuperman; Seth Long; Bears and the Option family; John Rogers; and Geoff Amthor.

Special thanks go to the gracious folks at the *Boston Globe*, which was the source of several quotes in the later chapters and of many of the pictures in the photo album section. I'm indebted to Muggsy Bogues for quotes from his book *In the Land of Giants*, published by Little, Brown and Co. I also want to acknowledge the assistance of the *Baltimore Sun* and *Sports Illustrated*.

Finally, I'm deeply grateful to all those who shared their memories of Reggie with me, and especially to his mother, Peggy Ritch. Without her help — and her trust — this story of Reggie's life could not have been told.

Preface

$\mathbb{A}$sk anyone who knew Reggie Lewis to describe him, and you are almost certain to hear "He was very quiet." Reggie had a warm smile. He rarely complained. He was content with simple pleasures. Even his mother would tell you "There wasn't really anything exciting in his life, other than basketball." But Reggie was more than just a great basketball player. He was a genuine, generous, caring young man with an intense dedication to improving himself and doing his best.

To understand Reggie, it is necessary to look beyond his basketball accomplishments to the less obvious strengths of his life and the forces that helped shape him as he was growing up. Poverty, drug use, and crime were commonplace in the Baltimore neighborhood where he was raised. Yet Reggie was able to steer clear of the dangers on the streets. He was blessed with a close, loving family and an extraordinary network of friends and mentors who offered him support and guidance throughout his life. He cherished his role models, and he took seriously his responsibility as a role model for others.

Reggie was often underestimated because of his unassuming nature. In a sport where flashy moves and outspoken stars get most of the attention, he had to earn respect the hard way: by constantly working to better his game. What he may have lacked in raw talent he more than made up for in discipline and determination.

Those who are looking for a further debate over the controversy surrounding Reggie's death will not find it here. The news reports of unproven allegations, medical speculation, and conflicting doctors' opinions should not be the lasting memory people hold of this superb athlete and wonderful human being. This book is not about the way Reggie Lewis died, but about the way he lived and about the lessons all of us — especially young people — can learn from his life.

Washington, D.C.   Craig Windham
March 1995

To Peggy Ritch,

a remarkable, loving mother

Reggie Lewis

Quiet Grace

Chapter One

Truck

The ball skipped once on the pavement before bounding back into Reggie Lewis's waiting hands. He wasted little time in firing off another pass, this time to his friend Damon Boyd. Damon caught the ball without breaking stride and weaved his way around a parked car and past the last defender in his path. Reggie raised his arms in the air: touchdown! "He could throw a football almost a whole block," Damon recalls. "I always thought his best sport was football." So did Reggie, for most of his childhood. Football was his favorite sport, and baseball was a close second.

Reggie liked to pitch. He had long arms, so he could really fire the ball. There was a playground nearby, but the neighborhood kids usually preferred to play in the streets or alleys or wherever else they could create a "ballpark." Reggie and his brother Irvin put boards end to end to boost themselves over a brick wall surrounding a courtyard at an industrial building. Once they were on the other side, they used the wall as a backstop for speedball, which they played using a stick of wood for a bat. Reggie's backyard provided its own special challenges. There was a food store next door. "Any ball hit onto the roof of the store was a home run," says Irvin, "but whoever hit it would have to figure out a way to retrieve the ball."

As a change of pace, Reggie occasionally shot baskets and played one-on-one, at the playground or in the yard. He and his brothers and friends would also play inside the house, shooting balls made of rolled-up socks at homemade goals. But it was not until Reggie was a teenager that he really focused on the sport that became his passion.

Reggie grew up in East Baltimore in a neighborhood of tidy row houses. His father, Irvin "Butch" Lewis, Sr., was what was known locally as an "Arab-er": he roamed the city with his horse and buggy selling fruits and vegetables. During the week, he would also buy and sell junk. Whenever he came upon appliances that worked or nice pieces of furniture, he would set them aside for use in his row house on Orleans Street. Butch met Reggie's mother, Inez (who is called "Peggy" by most of her relatives and friends) when she was only fourteen. He was her first love. Although they never married, Butch and Peggy lived together, off and on, for over eight years.

Peggy already had two children when she became pregnant again at the age of twenty. The strain began to take its toll. The bigger she got, the more her energy and her usually-positive attitude sagged. One Saturday, several of her girlfriends called her on the phone. "Come on! We don't like seeing you this down," they said. "We're going to do something about it." What they did was take Peggy to a nightclub, where she enjoyed an evening of music and dancing. She got home late that night, tired but happy.

5

The next evening, November 21, 1965, Peggy gave birth to Reggie at Baltimore City Hospital. He weighed seven pounds, five ounces. "He cried a lot when he was first born," Peggy says, "but he wound up being a good baby. He was plump and very smart; he walked early. Even as a baby, though, he was quiet and to himself."

Peggy now had the task of coping with three children. Sheron, the oldest, was as reserved as Reggie, but Irvin — a year-and-a-half Reggie's senior — was a handful. He was rambunctious and prone to mischief. Butch wasn't much help. When he was home, he was usually sleeping. "He was pretty much a street person," Peggy says. The kids all called him Butch. They liked him, but they considered him more of a friend than a father figure.

When Reggie was two, Peggy met a man named Benny Ritch, who was a merchant seaman. They fell in love and got married in 1968. Later that year, Peggy had her fourth child, Jon. He was born with a small hole in his heart, a condition that was repaired surgically when he was four years old.

Benny's work kept him away from the city for weeks on end. Still, the kids were closer to him than to Butch because he made a point of spending time with them whenever he was home. Peggy's marriage to Benny lasted only about a year. "It seems Butch was a part of me that I couldn't let go of," she says. Even after she broke up with Benny, however, he continued to support the children.

Peggy stayed home and raised not only her sons and daughter but also her younger sister, Cookie, who moved in at the age of twelve. "Our mother had died," Cookie says, "and it was just us: Peggy, me, our sisters Dot and Harriet, and our brother, Mickey. There was always a lot of love between us. There's nothing we wouldn't do for each other."

The family got by on welfare payments and food stamps. Peggy didn't work much when the children were young because she had heart problems, and she was concerned that a strenuous job could threaten her health. She had been diagnosed as having a heart murmur and leaky valves, and she had suffered a heart attack when she was seventeen. "Heart problems seemed to run in the family," she said.

An older woman who lived two doors away took an interest in Peggy and taught her how to cook and keep house. Her name was Edith Myers, and Peggy would run back and forth to her home constantly, to ask advice or just to chat. "She became like a mother to me," says Peggy. "My kids called her 'Aunt Edie,' and they thought of her children, Joyce, Vincent, Anthony, and Neal, as their cousins. They played together a lot."

Peggy's next door neighbor, Miss Craig, drove the children to Sunday school and church from time to time, but they never took a great interest in organized religion. Instead, Peggy talked to them about God and taught them how to say their prayers. She instilled in each of her children a deep respect for moral values.

Housekeeping may have been new to her, but Peggy had very definite ideas about the kind of home life she wanted to create for her children. She decided to give the kids as much freedom as possible — the kind of freedom she never had as a child. Peggy had rebelled against the restrictions imposed on her when she was young. "I figured that if I allowed my kids to do the things they wanted to do right at home, I wouldn't have to worry about them sneaking off and getting into trouble." Peggy told the children she would rather they stay in and around the house where she could keep an eye on them than roam the streets.

Peggy believes strongly that a house is meant to be lived in, not just looked at. As far as she was concerned, it was O.K. if the children ran in the house, or made noise, or even if they jumped on the beds. And they did a lot of jumping. In fact, they jumped so hard they broke the beds several times. The splintered slats and fractured bed frames would be dragged out to the curb. As soon as the beds were fixed, the bouncing began again. But Peggy didn't complain. She gave her children the freedom to do anything they wanted, within reason.

There were a few strict rules. Peggy would not allow the children to "hook" school. If they didn't want to go on a particular day, though, they were permitted to stay home as long as they remained inside the house until school was over. They were also expected to speak respectfully to adults, to do their chores, and to abide by whatever curfew Peggy set. Often they were told to be home before the streetlights came on. That was rarely a problem. "The kids didn't go out a lot," says Peggy. "They were never street types (except Irvin at times). They were real homebodies. Everything they wanted to do was there at the house."

What they liked to do most of all was watch television — Reggie and Sheron, especially. They would eat their meals or grab a snack and run right upstairs to their rooms. There, they would lounge around on their beds and watch TV for hours at a time. Adventure shows, westerns, movies: they loved them all. On Saturdays and Sundays, TV viewing often became a day-long affair. "When people were out looking for their kids," Peggy says, "I always knew right where mine were." Sometimes the children were so quiet she would forget they were even in the house.

When Reggie wasn't watching TV, he enjoyed all kinds of activities. He liked to roller skate and to do cartwheels and somersaults, but he was a little clumsy. He would always be falling and scraping his knees. The family played a lot of games together, including dominos and checkers, but card games were a specialty of the house. Their favorites ranged from Tunk to Pitty Pat.

Reggie created some imaginary friends when he was young, and he gave each of them a name. After his mother would put him down for a nap and leave the room, he'd lie in bed and talk to these friends and play with them. The laughter and chatter would be loud enough at times to be heard all the way downstairs. Peggy would go back up to find out what was going on. "He'd be in there talking to himself," she recalls. "I'd stick my head in the door and say, 'Boy, you'd better go to sleep! Who's in there with you?'"

Reggie was a skinny kid, but he had a huge appetite. "The boy could put down some food!" Peggy says. He loved crabs, peanut butter, grits, eggs, bacon, and cereal. But his favorite meal was fried chicken, potato salad, collard greens, and rice. The family had rice a lot, even at breakfast. It's one thing they could afford, and all the kids learned to like it.

At dinnertime, Cookie says, "Reggie would eat and eat, and whatever anyone left on their plate, he would eat that, too."

One evening when Reggie was no more than five years old, his stepfather, Benny, watched in amazement as he made the rounds at the dinner table. Reggie gobbled up the leftovers until each plate was clean. "Boy," Benny said, "you ain't nothing but a walking garbage truck!" Soon many of Reggie's relatives and friends began calling him "Truck." It was a nickname that would stay with him for the rest of his life.

Those years were happy ones for Peggy and the children. On sultry summer evenings, she gave the kids their baths and let them go outside to play with their friends. She sat on the porch, keeping an eye on them and relaxing, letting the stress of the day melt away. The last rays of the sunset would mingle with the city lights to cast a warm glow in the sky. If it was really hot, Peggy might go across the street to the corner bar and buy a pitcher of draft to bring home. She would sip the beer slowly as she read a romance novel. If the kids asked for a little taste, she would give them one. When it was time to go to bed, everyone went in together. The children would be tired by now, but they usually turned on the TV. Often they would fall asleep with it on.

The family moved frequently, but never very far. By the time Reggie was six years old, he had lived in six different row houses — nine by the time he went to college. All were within about four blocks of each other. The houses in the neighborhood had a variety of stone or painted brick fronts and entry steps made of marble blocks. In the back, there

were porches, compact yards, and narrow alleyways. The
families that lived on these streets took pride in the way the
neighborhood looked. They organized cleanups of the
sidewalks and alleys and kept flowers growing in window
boxes and planters in the summer.

Peggy had moving down to an art. She would throw a
party and invite her friends and relatives. They'd bring food
and cases of beer and do some socializing before getting
down to work. Her brother, Mickey, would borrow a truck
to transport the furniture and other heavy items. The guests
would also load up his white Pontiac with as much as it
could possibly hold. Then everyone would grab a couple of
boxes and carry them on foot to the new house, which was
never far away. The reason Peggy moved so often was to
improve the family's living situation. "Whenever I'd find
out that a better house nearby was available," she says, "I
would jump on it. Each home was nicer than the last. It
was always a new beginning, but, in a way, everything
stayed the same."

Because all the moves were concentrated in the same
neighborhood, the children never had to change schools.
Reggie wasn't very interested in studying, and he got average
grades until he became involved with basketball. In elementary school, he enjoyed classes where he could make things:
coasters, ashtrays, any kind of crafts. Reggie never liked
doing homework, but his mother insisted that it be finished
before he was allowed to go outside and play. So he did his
assignments as soon as he got home from school. Peggy
would check over the work, and if it wasn't right, he would
have to do it over before he went to bed.

Once all her children were in school, Peggy went out to look for a job so she could get off welfare. As for her heart condition, she decided "to stop nursing it and go on about living my life." Unfortunately, several employers told her they were unwilling to hire someone with heart problems. She eventually settled for a job as a waitress at a neighborhood bar.

When Peggy was at work, Cookie, who was now in high school, looked after the kids. She was very strict with all of them, except Jon, whom she admits she spoiled and protected. He would often talk back to his older brothers and needle them, and sometimes they would rough him up to teach him some respect. Jon knew how to have the last word, though. He would go crying to Cookie, and she would even the score quickly. To get the children to do their chores, all Peggy had to do was mention Cookie's name. "They were afraid of me!" Cookie chuckles.

Many children in the neighborhood were afraid of Reggie, too. He had a habit of hitting his head against walls — brick walls. He made a point of doing it while other kids were around. They'd wince as they watched. Afterwards, they would walk away telling each other, "Man, there's something wrong with Truck. He hits his head against walls," or "Truck's crazy. He'll butt you with his head! Don't mess with him." And they didn't. The head-banging was calculated, not crazy, Cookie says. "It was his way of keeping the guys off of him. That shows how smart he was. He didn't get in fights."

The same could not be said for Irvin. Fights were a regular occurrence for him. Unlike his brothers and sister,

Irvin had a bad temper, and he did not stick close to home. "I was on the streets," he says. "I was curious. I liked to explore. Now and then, I would get in a fight that looked like more than I could handle." When he did, Irvin would go running for home, usually with several bigger kids in hot pursuit. Peggy would not let him use the house as a refuge, though. She insisted that he stay outside until the situation was settled. But Reggie and Sheron were always ready to back up their brother — with a baseball bat that was kept just inside the front door. As Irvin reached the yard, they would rush outside brandishing the bat to scare away anyone who was giving him a hard time.

The children were disciplined when they misbehaved. Usually their TV time was cut·back, which was the worst possible punishment as far as they were concerned. Sometimes Peggy decided to administer a spanking. At least, she tried. She was a cigarette smoker then, and that habit plus her heart condition left her without much extra wind. "When it was time for me to spank them," Peggy says, "they would run around the beds in their rooms and get me so tired that I would finally call a halt and say, 'Look, you stop and sit down until I get my breath, and when I do I'm going to get you!' They would stop, but just for a second. Then they would start running around again and crawling over and under the beds." Very rarely did she catch them — or spank them.

Whenever possible, Peggy tried to choose a punishment to fit the offense. One day as she was walking up the street, she found Reggie and Irvin hiding underneath a car. They were attempting to smoke a cigar. Reggie was about eleven at the time. She ordered them to crawl out and stand up, and she marched them back to the house. There, she took the cigar, lit it, and made them smoke it right in front of her. "When it was Reggie's turn, he puffed a few times, then he started to cough and wheeze," she says. "He finally got sick and spit up all over my living room table. I don't think he ever smoked again." Peggy says she didn't have to discipline Reggie very often. "Any time he got into trouble, it was usually because Irvin had talked him into doing something, and it seems like every time they tried to pull a fast one, they got caught."

Graduation day at Collington Square Elementary School was a big event. The sixth grade class lined up for a formal procession into the auditorium to receive their diplomas. Reggie was dressed in a powder blue suit and dark open-collar shirt. All of the students posed for pictures afterwards. Later that day, his mother threw a surprise graduation party at the East Side Club, where she worked. Reggie and all his buddies were invited to come to the bar for sodas and snacks. "They were so excited," Peggy says. "They played the jukebox and sat on the bar stools and whirled around and had a big old time."

Every weekend Peggy's entire family got together. In the summertime, they liked to jam into two cars and drive to Carr's Beach or Sandy Point at the Chesapeake Bay or to a city park. More often, they would gather Friday night at one home or another for a dinner of fish, cornbread, grits, and greens. Peggy says her house was the favorite of the children "because they could go buck wild. All of the kids could come to Miss Peggy's house and jump on the darn beds!" While the kids were jumping, the adults were playing card games.

Reggie became a very good card player himself, thanks to a lot of practice with his brothers and sister and friends. He also liked to pitch cards and coins. The object was to see who could get closest to a step or the brick wall of the house without touching it. All the kids in the neighborhood would pitch, usually pennies and quarters. Reggie's long reach gave him an advantage. It didn't take long before he had won enough change to buy himself some new sneakers.

Peggy saved as much as she could, which was usually very little. After putting aside money for months one year, she managed to surprise each of her children with the gift of a bicycle. Reggie loved the blue bike his mother gave him. Blue was his favorite color. He rode the bike almost nonstop the first day, showing it off to all his friends. But that was the only day he had it. He leaned it against the front of a store for just a few seconds while he ran in to buy some candy. When he came out, the bike was gone. Reggie was stunned. He walked home slowly. As he told his mother what had happened, tears welled up in his eyes. "I doubt if I ever get another bike," he said.

"He knew it had taken a lot to get those bikes," Peggy says. "That thing hurt him some kind of bad."

Such displays of emotion were rare for Reggie. He kept his feelings mainly to himself. Most of the time he was good-natured and happy. "He never really got upset," Jon recalls. "He never had a temper."

Peggy says Reggie was very sensitive, though. "He would cry in a heartbeat," she says. One of the most emotional events of his childhood involved a pet. When he was about thirteen, Reggie told his mother that he wanted a dog. "A dog is a lot of responsibility," she replied. "You would have to clean up after it, and walk it, and take care of it every day."

"I will Mama! I promise I will," he said. So Peggy got her son a cute, brown puppy, which he named Butch. And Reggie kept his word: he did everything to care for the dog. He really loved Butch.

One afternoon Reggie wanted to go to Collington Square with some of his friends to play baseball, so he put a choke chain and leash on the dog and tied him to the stairs in the basement. Butch was only about two months old and full of energy. After Reggie left, the puppy ran up and down the staircase, testing the limits of the leash. Suddenly one of his paws slipped, and he rolled through the opening at the back of the stairs. As Butch fell, the chain pulled tight around his neck, and he was unable to free himself. The dog choked to death.

When Jon discovered Butch, he rushed over to the park to tell his brother. Reggie was at bat, waiting for the next pitch. He was cranky because he wasn't hitting well. Jon ran up to him and shouted, "You've got to come home right away!" Reggie was annoyed at the intrusion and shoved him aside. "Listen to me!" Jon insisted. Again Reggie pushed his brother out of his way. Finally, Jon blurted out what had happened: "Butch is dead!" Reggie's eyes widened with shock, and his jaw went slack. The baseball bat dropped from his hands and kicked up a puff of dust as it hit the ground.

And he began to cry.

Reggie and Jon sprinted home. Once they got there, word of Butch's fate spread quickly. As the other family members were told about the accident, they, too, started crying. Peggy had never seen Reggie so upset. To soothe some of the emotional pain, she suggested that they have a funeral for the puppy. So later that day, everyone gathered in the back yard. A small grave was dug, and Butch was laid to rest. Peggy says the loss had a big impact on her son:

"That was the first and last time Reggie ever asked me for anything."

Chapter Two

A Place Called Cecil-Kirk

Reggie never showed much interest in basketball until his older brother decided to start taking him to the outdoor court at Collington Square, where all the neighborhood kids played. Irvin admits he had an ulterior motive for bringing him along. "I first took Reggie to Collington because he was tall, and I knew he could get rebounds and pass off to me so I would get more shots. He was good even then, and the more people saw that, the more they wanted him on their team."

Irvin was an excellent basketball player, and the brotherly rivalry that developed helped motivate Reggie to improve. "Reggie would compete against him and try to get better and better so he could beat him," says Jon. "That drove Reggie even harder."

The Collington Square court was lighted all night long. To avoid the sweltering summer heat, Reggie and Irvin would wait until midnight to play — with their mother's blessing. "There weren't as many people on the courts then, and it was much cooler," she says. "I never worried about sending them out that late at night. It wasn't a bad neighborhood, and Reggie was a good kid."

Reggie played on a Collington Square recreation team one summer, but that was the extent of his organized basketball experience until Sheron began dating a young man named Joe Dickens, who was about nineteen at the time. Joe took an immediate interest in Reggie. "I play basketball. So anytime I see a kid who is big as well as young enough to have time to grow and develop, I try to help them out." Reggie certainly fit the bill: he was 6 feet 4 inches tall even though he was just fourteen years old. On his visits to see Sheron, Joe made a point of speaking to Reggie. He talked to him more each day. Sometimes he'd strike up a conversation while Reggie was watching sports on TV. "For him to be sitting around doing nothing seemed like a waste," says Joe. "Slowly but surely, I got him talking about basketball. Eventually he said he wanted to play some ball."

Out on the court, Joe sized up Reggie's talent, and he liked what he saw. Reggie was a pure shooter, even at fourteen. "It was a gift," says Joe. "Everything else he had to work on, including defense and ball-handling. I ran basic drills with him and taught him passing, dribbling, and how to box out." Joe was an aggressive, physical player, and that's the way he taught Reggie to be. "He was pushed around some at the start," Joe says, "but once he learned how to push back, it was never a problem. He got respect as soon as he walked on the court." Joe had always regretted not taking up the sport himself until he was fifteen. That's one reason he was eager to work with Sheron's brother. Reggie was also getting a late start, but it was not too late, especially if he immersed himself in the game.

Joe began taking Reggie to different communities every day to give him a chance to play against a wide variety of people — people he didn't know. "When you play with the same folks day in and day out," Joe says, "you don't have any incentive to improve. You just laugh and shoot and run up and down the court. It's a clown's game. But because we were playing in lots of places, Reggie didn't know his opponents, so he didn't joke around with them. He was serious." Every night was a new challenge.

Not only was Reggie exposed to all sorts of playing styles, but also to different attitudes. "A lot of time when you play street ball," Joe says, "guys wind up fighting because they don't know how to adjust to all the tough talk. They let it bother them. That's the way basketball is: if people can get under your skin, they'll do it. But I would prepare Reggie. I'd tell him, 'People are going to say this and that, but you let it go in one ear and out the other, and just keep playing the game.'" Reggie learned that lesson well. He gained the ability to ignore what his opponents said. No matter how much they tried to anger him or rattle him, they never got to him. "At first, other players would say things to try to intimidate Reggie," Joe says, "but he always kept his cool. He never got into fights. Afterwards, many of those same people would come up to Reggie and tell him, 'Nice game.'"

Joe's forays with Reggie to different parts of the city became an almost daily ritual. After school, they would play for at least an hour or two most days, and all day on weekends. "There were times when he said he'd rather not go," Joe recalls. "I might spend an hour convincing him to come along rather than staying glued to the TV, even if it was just to watch me. Once we got there, he would usually play."

Reggie had twin cousins, Terry and Perry Dozier, who lived in Columbia, Maryland, south of Baltimore. Much to Joe's surprise, they were even taller than Reggie although they were a year younger. "They weren't playing much," Joe says, "so I would call them and drive Reggie out there. The four of us spent many an afternoon playing." The twins were supposed to stay in the house until their mother got home from work, but they would come out anyway. They also started joining Reggie and Joe and occasionally Irvin on their trips to different playgrounds around Baltimore. "As long as they wanted to go," Joe says, "I would take them."

The more Reggie played, the more confidence he gained in his ability. "I talked to him, played along side him, and told him things he had to do to improve his game," says Joe, "and he went out and did it." In several games on the West Side, which has a reputation as the rough part of town, Reggie hit the winning bucket. Some of those who played against him would come up to him after a game and say, "Hey, Slim, why don't you all come back next week?"

Joe felt it was time for Reggie to play more than street ball, so he took him to a recreation center that was some distance from Reggie's neighborhood. The Cecil-Kirk Multipurpose Center was named after two of the streets that border it. Joe had played on a team there, and he knew that it had an excellent basketball program. He introduced Reggie to one of the leaders of the center, Anthony Lewis (no relation), whose nickname is "Doody." "I talked to

Doody about putting Reggie on a team to see what he could do," Joe says.

Reggie landed an immediate starting role as center because of his size, but shortly after he began playing at Cecil-Kirk he was ready to quit the team. He told his mother he was upset because he thought he should be getting the ball more often. He felt ignored in the offense. When Reggie failed to show up for practice, Anthony and another coach from the center, Calvin Dotson, paid him a visit. They asked him why he was unhappy, and they told him they wanted him back. They also talked to Peggy and asked her to intervene, but she said if Reggie didn't want to play, nobody could make him.

The next evening when Joe came to see Sheron, he stopped by Reggie's room. He found him lying in bed watching TV. As he frequently did, Joe flopped down across the bottom of the bed and started a conversation. It didn't take long before Reggie had spelled out all of his frustrations and criticisms of the Cecil-Kirk team. "I told him that even though things may not seem to be going his way," Joe says, "that was no reason to be a quitter. I advised him to talk to the coaches and tell them his concerns. That's what they were there for." Joe promised that if Reggie talked to the coaches and nothing changed, Joe would talk to them himself.

Reggie rejoined the team, but it wasn't long before he had decided to quit again. "He was frustrated with some of the game situations," Joe says. "He still felt he wasn't getting the ball enough, or the guys weren't passing it to him. I heard him out and told him if he just stayed focused

on playing his best, things would get better. He had to earn
the trust and respect of his teammates." How did Reggie
react to this advice? "It wasn't easy to read him," Joe says.
"Reggie was always cool. He showed little emotion. He
would just say, 'All right, man.' But I'm convinced that if
we had not had those talks, he wouldn't have played."

Reggie went back to Cecil-Kirk — this time for good.
Getting comfortable with organized team play took some
time, but he finally adjusted and began to enjoy himself and
to look forward to practices. From the recreation center he
would walk across an expanse of grass and blacktop to a
small, windowless school gymnasium barely large enough for
one basketball court. The wooden floor was dark from years
of refinishing. It was here that Cecil-Kirk teams played, and
it was here that Reggie Lewis showed his first real devotion
to the game that would shape his life.

It was the shape of his body that had finally convinced
Reggie that football was not his sport. He was skinny, and
his lack of bulk left him vulnerable to injury. "There was a
time when Reggie was playing a game at Hollandtown,"
recalls his brother Jon. "He got hit and hurt. After that, I
remember him saying he wasn't going to play football
anymore. He was too slender. By then everyone was telling
him that basketball was his game."

Reggie got more and more involved with his Cecil-Kirk
team, and soon he began spending most of his after-school
hours at the center. The squat brick building was an oasis
for hundreds of kids. Joyce Venable and the other staff
members scurried about, keeping tabs on the different
activities, and Anthony was a constant and commanding

presence. He answered phone calls, settled arguments, joked with the kids, and offered encouragement. Anthony became more than just a coach to Reggie; he was also a lifelong mentor and friend.

The youngest children would arrive at Cecil-Kirk at about three o'clock. Older students showed up later in the afternoon. The kids would spend the first hour or so just unwinding: shooting pool, playing ping-pong, or watching videos. By five o'clock, the Center was bustling with activity. The sound was a mixture of voices, laughter, and music, punctuated by the loud klaxon horn that blared when the telephone in the office rang. Before the time set aside each day for doing homework, many of the young people went to the carry-out next door to grab a snack.

The sign over the store entrance says "Roman's Food Market," but everyone in the neighborhood calls the place "Woody's," after the soft-spoken man who has worked behind the deli counter for decades, frying chicken and making sandwiches. Woody Venable (Joyce's father) says Reggie and his friends would usually order cheese/fish subs or cheeseburgers and fries plus soft drinks. "If they didn't have enough money, I trusted them to pay me later, and they never let me down. They were good kids." As for Reggie, Woody says, "He was very nice. You couldn't find a better person than he."

The Cecil-Kirk teams practiced on weekday evenings and played games against other recreation center teams on weekends. After his own practice was finished, Reggie would sometimes stay around to watch the older kids play before heading home. He would make the trip by bus or get a ride. Reggie never seemed to mind the long days.

As his basketball skills improved, Reggie's interest in the game grew into a full-scale passion. His mother says, "It came on him all of a sudden. He ate, slept, and breathed basketball. It became everything to him."

Reggie's body was cooperating: his coordination was noticeably better. "He finally had control of his limbs," Anthony says. "That's when he became a little more aggressive about the sport."

Anthony also became aware of something different about the way Reggie approached the game. His attitude "began to change and mature — the time he would put into his practice." Reggie continued to play at different playgrounds with Joe and Terry and Perry. Even at home, he looked for every opportunity to refine his shot. There always seemed to be a game going in the backyard or alley. The kids fashioned makeshift baskets out of milk crates and attached them to fences or trees at the perfect height for dunking.

One secret to Reggie's rapid growth as a player was the fact that he was a quick study. "He may have been quiet," says Joe, "but he did a lot of listening. You could tell him something, and he would catch on right away. Whatever mistake he might have been making, he would go out on the court and change it." He didn't have a lot to fix, though. Joe says, "Reggie was already gifted when he started playing the game, he was just unaware of it." Developing those skills was just a matter of time and discipline.

Reggie had a goal: he wanted to play varsity basketball with Irvin at Patterson High School, and he was sure he was now good enough to make the squad. But the coach had a different opinion. He didn't think much of Reggie's ability, and he cut him from the team before the season began. Irvin says, "I always wanted to play with Reggie on the same team, but none of the coaches — from high school to college — seemed to want us together. My middle name is Mack; his nickname was 'Truck.' Together we would have been like a Mack Truck: unstoppable." While Irvin was disappointed, Reggie was devastated by the coach's action. Again, he was considering giving up basketball completely when Anthony sat him down for the first of what would be several similar talks over the years.

Anthony knows how to communicate with young people, and, like Joe, he had a great rapport with Reggie. "You had to know him as a person, and if you did, you knew he would reject any harsh handling of a situation. The key to kids is: are they paying attention to you? You read the riot act to some kids, but with Reggie, a stern but low-keyed approach worked. If you were harsh, you would run him away, and in this game you want your players to run to you, not away from you."

As he sat in Anthony's office, Reggie talked about how surprised he had been by the coach's action, which he felt was unfair. Anthony tried to redirect Reggie's attention toward the future and to put the situation in perspective. Being cut was not the end of the world, or a basketball career. "You sometimes need someone to pick you up and say, 'Things are not as bad as they seem to be,'" Anthony says. "You're not as good as you think you are when things are going great, and you're not as bad as you think when things are going terribly." Reggie listened carefully as Anthony told him that nothing in life comes easy. "If you want it, it's there for you to get, but you have to go after it."

Anthony outlined in detail what Reggie would have to do if he wanted to improve his game, and Reggie rose to the challenge. He began practicing more intently. "The basketball became his best friend," according to Jon. "It was with him wherever he went. Even when he walked to the store, he had that basketball."

What set Reggie apart from other kids was not his talent but his work ethic, in Anthony's opinion. Most kids would try to cut corners. Not Reggie. "If you told him he needed to go to the gym and work on his jump shot fifty times," Anthony says, "you could rest assured that he would do it."

There were dozens of rec centers like Cecil-Kirk in Baltimore, and the competition among their various teams was intense. The games offered a preview of a host of future college and professional stars. Reggie and David Wingate were just two of the standouts on the team from Cecil-Kirk. "This is where it all started," says Herman "Tree" Herried, who later played with Reggie in high school. There was more to Cecil-Kirk than basketball, though. Herried says, "Guys like Anthony groomed us, along with our parents, to become good people."

A fierce rivalry developed between Cecil-Kirk and the team from Lafayette, which featured another Reggie, Reggie "Russ" Williams, and Tyrone "Muggsy" Bogues. "Those games were special," Muggsy recalls. "We were just out there to have fun and play hard and beat each other's butts. Russ and Muggs against Truck and 'Gate. We were the talk of the city." Reggie enjoyed the games immensely. Whenever he dunked the ball on someone, he would run back up the court with a big grin on his face.

During the summer, Reggie played in the Baltimore Neighborhood Basketball League (BNBL), a highly-competitive program that attracts the city's best players. That is where he caught the eye of Bob Wade, the coach at Dunbar High School, who attended BNBL games to look for young talent. Wade saw promise in the lanky teenager, and Anthony put in a good word for Reggie. "He told me that he felt the kid could play," Wade says. "He also told me that Reggie wasn't given a good look at Patterson High." Knowing of Wade's interest, Anthony began suggesting to Reggie that he consider transferring to Dunbar, which had both an excellent basketball program and a highly-regarded curriculum in health services.

Besides playing in different city leagues, Reggie was offered a paid summer job at Cecil-Kirk as a counselor to younger children. To qualify for the federally-funded position, he had to get a physical exam. The doctor who checked him over paused as he listened to Reggie's chest. "You have a heart murmur," he said. "It is caused by turbulent blood flow through the heart. I can hear the sound clearly through the stethoscope." In talking to Reggie and his mother, the doctor insisted that the condition was not serious, and he assured them that Reggie would eventually grow out of it completely.

Reggie really enjoyed his job. He loved working with kids, and he was earning some badly-needed spending money, which made the summer a lot more fun. Several of his friends were also counselors. They all took great delight in hanging out with the Center staff members and playing practical jokes on them.

One of the senior leaders at Cecil-Kirk was a woman who was responsible for organizing and chaperoning field trips for the children, with help from Reggie and the other counselors. She was a bit high-strung, and she took her responsibility seriously, sometimes too seriously, the counselors thought. She would carefully check her list as the bus left Cecil-Kirk. "O.K., we've got 32 kids," she would say. On the way back, though, she would rely on the counselors to do the counting, and they made sure the numbers never quite added up. Usually they conspired to come up one or two short. Sometimes, however, when everyone appeared to be on the bus and accounted for, the counselors would say, "Ma'am, there are still three kids in the bathroom." Either way, the leader launched into a frenzy of double-checking as Reggie and his fellow counselors did their best to stifle their laughter. It usually took several minutes before she realized they had been pulling her leg.

After considering all of his options, Reggie decided to abandon his dream of playing with Irvin at Patterson and to transfer to Dunbar. There, he would be assured of playing on the varsity. When Anthony called Coach Wade to sound him out, Wade was enthusiastic. Unlike the Patterson coach, Wade saw something different in Reggie. "I saw that he could play the game," Wade says. "He ran the floor well, he had great hands, he had outstanding leaping ability, and he had a good nose for the basketball. He impressed me both as a youngster and as an athlete."

Reggie remained a young man of few words. He let his ever-present smile and his moves on the basketball court do most of his talking for him, and he devoted himself to honing his skills. The game became more than just a sport to him. "Reggie used basketball as his escape route," Jon says. "A lot of things would build up inside him, and he'd go shoot baskets."

Another outlet for Reggie was spending time with his sister, Sheron. They were very close — "like SuperGlue," according to Joe. "Sheron and Reggie were both so quiet," remembers their mother. They did everything together — watched TV, played cards, went to the movies — and yet they would barely say a word. For them, a long conversation would be:

"Sheron, that movie was good."

"Uh huh."

Martial arts movies were their favorites; those starring Bruce Lee were at the top of the list. Reggie and Sheron would often go to a neighborhood theater that showed four kung fu and karate films for a dollar. They would stay there for hours, enjoying all the action. Along with Irvin, Reggie even studied martial arts for a while. They managed to persuade a man who knew some karate to come to their house and teach them different moves in the basement. "He was crippled," Irvin recalls, "but he could break bricks with his hands, and that was enough to impress us. We really got into it."

When he wasn't playing ball, Reggie usually stayed close to home. He had no real interest in exploring the streets like his brother Irvin. "Reggie was not the type of person who would hang just to be hangin'," Joe says. For Reggie, hanging out meant spending time in his room or across the street at his friend Larry's house. Reggie also enjoyed clowning around with his brothers and gently teasing his big sister. He noticed that Sheron had taken a liking to Elvis Presley. So whenever Reggie would spot Elvis on TV, he would say: "Hey Sheron, your boyfriend's on."

The appetite that had earned Reggie the nickname "Truck" got even bigger during his teenager years. He was always raiding the kitchen for a bite to eat. One snack he came to really like was Cap'n Crunch cereal, but it was only an occasional treat. Peggy couldn't afford to shell out several dollars for a box of cereal too often.

Peggy insisted that all of her children do chores around the house. A list was posted on the refrigerator each week assigning the different tasks, including emptying the trash, washing dishes, sweeping the front steps, and vacuuming the floors. None of them appealed to Reggie, according to his mother, "especially washing dishes. He hated that. He would make deals with his sister and brothers to get out of doing chores." Sometimes Sheron and Reggie would swap responsibilities; sometimes they would just pay each other to do a job. The going rate for the dreaded dish-washing: about two dollars.

Money was always a scarce resource in Peggy Ritch's household, and Reggie knew it. "He never liked you to make a fuss over him," she says. The boys had to have new tennis shoes every other month, because their feet were growing so fast. If Reggie and either Jon or Irvin needed shoes at the same time, Reggie would pick out a cheap pair. He would tell his mother, "You get them the good ones, and I'll wear these."

By the end of the year, the family's finances were often stretched even further than usual. At Christmas, Reggie would tell Peggy, "Get gifts for Irvin, Jon, and Sheron first. You can get something for me later." Reggie always wanted to be the last. But Peggy did not want any of her children to feel last — or left out. She would give them some money to buy gifts for each other. Reggie and Jon would often buy her some costume jewelry.

One Christmas, Peggy wanted to surprise the family with something different. She decided to get one large gift that all of the kids could share: a full-sized pool table. "It was a big old nice table," she says. "I paid a lot for it." Rather than relegating it to the basement, Peggy cleared out the dining room, and set it up there. The pool table instantly became the center of attention in a home where kids had always been encouraged to play and have fun. "Everybody liked to come to our house because they could have a ball," Peggy says. Reggie loved the table, and he became quite good at shooting pool.

Despite a lack of money, the kids had gifts every Christmas. The family was poor, but they were never deprived — of toys or clothes for school. The kids were never made to feel they had to do without anything. Just feeding four growing children, however, was a challenge for Peggy. "All of our families ate well at the beginning of a month," says Reggie's Aunt Cookie. "That's when we would get a new batch of food stamps. Then we would help each other out whenever any of our supplies ran low."

Peggy needed help when she came home one day and discovered that someone had broken into her freezer. All of the food had been stolen. "Peggy never believed in locking doors," says Cookie. Relatives chipped in and gave Peggy enough groceries to tide her over until the next allotment of food stamps arrived.

"We had more rice than usual that month," Peggy remembers with a smile.

Reggie and his brothers and sister developed a deep appreciation for their mother's resourcefulness and her willingness to sacrifice for them. "We had tough times," Reggie later recalled, "but there were good times, too. More good times than bad times."

Peggy's brother, Mickey, marvels at the way she managed to make do, in all sorts of difficult circumstances. "Peggy made her way out of no way," he says. "She never left her children without food — or love."

Chapter Three

Dunbar Days

Reggie approached his transfer to Dunbar High School with a mixture of excitement and apprehension. He was more than halfway through his tenth grade year when he changed schools, so the transition was not as easy as it might otherwise have been. His classmates had already had several months to get to know each other. He was convinced he had made the right decision, however, and it wasn't long before he was making new friends.

Dunbar's hulking, modern buildings are wedged like stacks of blocks amid low-rise housing projects, directly across Caroline Street from the sprawling Johns Hopkins University Hospital complex. The school was named after Paul Laurence Dunbar, a famous African-American poet who died in 1906, so the basketball team is known as the Poets. Dunbar has a reputation in Baltimore as a school that not only produces excellent athletes but also offers a solid education.

Coach Wade is an imposing man who once played professional football under the legendary Vince Lombardi. Like Lombardi, he considers discipline the key to success — in sports or life. "I told Reggie and all of my players they had to abide by the Wade Rule: go to class, do your best academically, turn assignments in on time, be at practice on time, and don't make excuses." Reggie knew that he would have to keep his grades up to stay on the team. He started to put more effort into his school work.

Reggie clearly liked his health services courses the best. This was a specialty at Dunbar, a "magnet" curriculum that drew students from all over the city. In one class, Reggie learned how to make dentures. "He enjoyed working with his hands," Peggy says, "and just as with basketball, if there was something he liked, he put his all into it." Reggie would bring some of the dentures he made home to show them off. "You could see the proudness in his face," Peggy says. "He would say, 'Look, mom. Look what I did!'"

A girl from Reggie's dental class came up to him one day in the cafeteria and said she knew someone who wanted to meet him: a friend of hers named Taresa Stewart. "I had noticed him in the hallways," says Taresa. "What caught my eye was his blue-and-white Cecil-Kirk jacket. I couldn't bring myself to talk to him because I was kind of shy, so I asked my friend to introduce us." Taresa quickly learned that Reggie was even more reserved than she was. "He was quiet and very, *very* shy. He was so quiet that he even made me nervous initially." Taresa had a feeling that Reggie liked her, although he didn't exactly say so at first. Eventually, they became more comfortable talking with each other, and they started dating.

Taresa became Reggie's first real girl friend. On dates, they went out to the movies or on roller skating trips with Taresa's community association (although Reggie usually didn't skate). They also frequently traveled downtown by bus or cab to Harbor Place, the city's waterfront area. After dinner at Phillip's Crab House, they would get some ice cream and take a long stroll along the harbor promenade.

"I liked Reggie because he was sweet, kind, and very understanding," Taresa says. "Most guys just wanted to be intimate, but he wasn't that type of person. He cared about me for me. We were best friends. He didn't let anybody bother me, but he wasn't overly protective. He didn't try to keep me under lock and key. He let me have the freedom to be myself."

Reggie and Taresa began spending more and more time with each other. She would sometimes cut one of her own courses so she could sit in on his dental class and watch him work. They even studied together. On many school nights, Taresa would be at Reggie's house until ten or eleven o'clock doing History or English or working on a report. Then Reggie would walk her to the bus; they lived on opposite sides of town. When Taresa got home, she'd often call Reggie, and they would talk on the phone for hours, making plans for the next day.

Taresa says it wasn't long before she and Reggie were inseparable. Taresa's mother, Beverly, puts it another way: "When you saw him, you saw her. They were joined at the hip. If they weren't at his house, they were at ours," Beverly says. She was concerned about them keeping their grades up because they were together so much on school nights, but Beverly insists she never minded the relationship. "Reggie was the type of person who, if you met him, you couldn't help but like him," she says. "He was a very respectful young man. He was mild-mannered and lovable — his disposition never changed."

On some of the evenings Reggie was at Taresa's, she would sneak him down into her basement so he could sleep there and not have to make the long trip home. One night, Beverly discovered that he was there and called Peggy to make sure it was O.K. for him to stay over. "The next morning I invited him up for breakfast," Beverly says. "He ate like there was no tomorrow. I felt like I was feeding the whole basketball team."

By the fall of 1981, Reggie was eager for Dunbar's season to begin. He was not able to join the team as a sophomore because of his midyear transfer. Through the spring and summer he had continued playing at Cecil-Kirk and in various city leagues, from BNBL to Project Survival. He had spent a lot of time working on his game, and now he was ready to show what he could do at the high school level.

The Poets had a long winning tradition. They had only lost three games the previous year, but the '81-'82 season promised to be even better. Several of the talented teenagers who had played against each other in the recreation leagues were now going to be on the same team. Besides Reggie, there were Reggie Williams, David Wingate, Muggsy Bogues, Tim Dawson, Gary Graham, Keith James, Tree Herried, Darryl Wood, and Derrick Lewis, just to name a few. Coach Wade did his best to unify them. He insisted that they always travel to and from away games together on the bus. "If they would argue or make fun of one another," he says, "I would step in and say, 'You guys can't be successful when there is a separation.' I just kept preaching family to them." And hard work.

Wade had a reputation for putting his players through long, tough practices. "He'd bring out sandbags and bricks and make us run suicide drills, dragging the bags or carrying the bricks in our hands," Muggsy recalls. "We'd run with those bricks, and if anyone dropped one, we'd have to start the whole darn thing over again." By the end of practice, the players would often be gasping for air.

At first, Wade questioned Reggie's stamina and his speed. He did not consider him to be the best basketball player on the team, but he did regard him as one of the most consistent and reliable. Wade says Reggie was a coach's dream. "You didn't have to go over things repeatedly with him. He retained information well. He was eager to learn, he would always listen, and when it was time for him to perform, he did. He would do what he was asked." Wade felt Reggie's most important quality, though, was that he would never complain.

Reggie usually had the task of playing Reggie Williams head-to-head in practice. "Russ" was already being touted as the number one prep player in the country. Wade says the two had very different playing styles. "Reggie didn't have the graceful moves or the rotation the Kid had on his shot. Reggie had a side spin on his ball. Russ had a topspin on his." They would be on opposing squads during practice. Reggie more than held his own, and he earned respect in the process. "It was fun, real fun," Reggie recalled, "The toughest competition we had was among each other at practice. We would really go at each other. I mean, it was a war."

The difficult practices began paying off, bringing the players together as a team. "We had no ego problems," Muggsy says. "We loved each other like brothers, and I think the rest of the school respected us for that. We looked out for each other." Coach Wade looked out for his players, too. He lectured them about avoiding kids who would get them in trouble, and he had help in making sure they didn't slip up.

People in the community knew of Wade's disciplined approach to dealing with kids, and they supported him. If they saw any of the players hanging out with the wrong crowd, they would call him and let him know. It was as if he had a whole network of informants working for him. And Wade didn't hesitate to challenge his players with what he learned.

"He'd say, 'I understand you weren't in class today,' or 'You were seen hanging out with so-and-so,'" says Muggsy. "If it was true, he would punish the whole team. He'd make us run with the bricks and sandbags. If we ever asked why we were being punished, he'd say, 'Ask your teammate so-and-so. He'll tell you why.'" The resulting peer pressure plus the public humiliation was more than enough to make the players think twice about violating the Coach's commandments. Reggie didn't need any incentive to steer clear of trouble. He seemed to have an innate ability throughout his life to identify people who were up to no good and to stay away from them.

Reggie was originally slated to be on the starting team at Dunbar, but the day before the first game he suffered a cut in practice that required stitches. "I was supposed to start," Reggie said. "I thought I should have started, but after I got hurt, Coach Wade put Tim Dawson in instead." Dawson played well, so he stayed in the lineup, even after Reggie's cut had healed. Reggie was relegated to a reserve role. He became known as "the sixth man." Reggie was disappointed, but he never told Coach Wade.

Home games at Dunbar were electric. There was always a standing-room-only crowd jammed in so tightly that the floor would sweat from the humidity. Up in the rafters of the gym were rows of banners and pennants — over two dozen of them — representing city titles, undefeated seasons, and national championships. The cheers were deafening when the players sprinted onto the court in their maroon, gold, and white uniforms. Even in pregame warmups, the Poets would put on a show: they ran a dazzling, precision layup line with alley-oops and dunks galore. If the opponents weren't intimidated before the opening tip, they were shortly afterward. Dunbar had depth and discipline. The Poets would put together lopsided stretches where they would outscore the other team by a ten-to-one margin. The cheerleaders kept the fans in a frenzy:

Dribble Dribble
Shoot Shoot
Take that ball to the Hoop, Hoop, Hoop!
Go, Fight, Win!
Shake that thing!

The team was victorious in game after game. "We were winning. We were *it*," says Muggsy. "I mean playing in the NBA is fun, but it's different. In high school, we couldn't lose. We couldn't even *imagine* losing. We killed everyone."

Being a reserve at Dunbar was no disgrace. The Poets' bench was better than most starting teams in the city. But Reggie was frustrated by his lack of playing time. He sat patiently, waiting for his turn. When the Coach did finally put him in, Reggie felt under pressure to play perfectly. If he made a mistake, he was often quickly yanked out of the game. He thought that was unfair, but again he kept his feelings to himself. While he didn't voice his opinion to the Coach, he did talk with Taresa. Sometimes *she* talked to the Coach on Reggie's behalf. "I'd say, 'Why did you take him out? He made one mistake and you take him out! You know you're wrong.'"

Wade disagreed, but he seemed impressed by Taresa's outspokenness. "This girl can talk!" he would say.

It wasn't just being a backup that disturbed Reggie. He also bristled over the way Coach Wade treated him in practice. Wade challenged his players to improve by nagging and teasing them. "You don't have a jumper," he would tell Reggie.

"I can outshoot you, Coach."

"But you don't have a jump shot."

"I'll bet I can outshoot you, though."

Reggie and the Coach would have shooting contests after practice, and Reggie would stay even later to work on his release and his quick-dribble jump-stop shot. "He was engrossed in proving to me that he had that shot," Wade says. The Coach wasn't satisfied, though, so the pestering continued. It carried over into games.

While Reggie was running past the bench during one of his brief appearances, he heard the Coach say, "That is the ugliest jump shot in the nation." Reggie rolled his eyes in response. When he was playing in a game, Reggie was totally focused. He would hear only one person: the coach. "Reggie paid no attention to anyone else," says his friend Joe. "No one could ever distract him when he was on the court."

Reggie answered Wade's challenge. He sank one of the key shots of the game, and it was a jumper. As he passed the bench, he looked squarely at the Coach and said, "I have a jump shot."

Wade smiled. "It showed me the determination he had as a player."

The Poets had a signature play they liked to run toward the end of a quarter as the clock was winding down. The Coach would showcase one of his star players. "I'd move the guards to the side and give Russ the ball," Wade says. "He'd have the option of going one-on-one or penetrating and kicking it out to a shooter in the corner." Reggie decided he wanted a taste of this spotlight, and he told the Coach. Wade saw another opportunity to prod his sixth man toward a goal.

"You're not a dribbler," he said.

Reggie set to work on improving his ball-handling skills. He put plastic cones out on the court after practice and dribbled around them. He did drills to increase his control and speed. His efforts were rewarded: the Coach put him in the showcase position several times. "We let him be the center of attention," Wade says. "He responded with good ball handling, and he made good decisions."

Reggie let his actions on the court do his speaking for him. He wasn't trying to impress the Coach; he just wanted his respect. When Reggie slammed home a dunk, he would look at Wade and ask, "How do you like me now?"

So the Coach's motivational tactics worked. Despite Reggie's improvement, however, he remained a reserve player. And what Wade regarded as good-natured teasing, Reggie sometimes saw as taunting. One remark in particular stung him. Wade told Reggie, "You aren't going to be anything but a Division II player in college." At first, Reggie resented the statement, but it lingered in his mind for years. He was intent on eventually proving Coach Wade wrong.

Reggie always felt he had something to prove. Because of his quiet manner, he was often underestimated, but he had a deep sense of self-confidence. He never really doubted himself. When he didn't play as well as he might have liked, he looked forward to the next game. He had faith in his ability, and he was certain he was good enough to be a starter.

His friends agreed and did their best to boost his spirits. I would tell him, "'Everything happens for a reason,'" Taresa says. "'Whenever you get in there, show them what you can do.'" Joe advised him to keep going to practice and playing hard. Sooner or later, he told Reggie, the coach would have to put him in. It wasn't long, though, before

Reggie became increasingly disillusioned over his lack of playing time.

His frustrations finally came to a head after an especially grueling practice. It was a day Reggie would never forget. "Coach was dogging me. He was calling me lazy and telling me I didn't have a work ethic. It wasn't true, but he just wanted to have something to say. He kept subbing out everyone but me. He was leaving me out there to die. And I *was* dying, but I didn't let him see that. I wasn't going to let him beat me."

Reggie made it through the practice. He put on his sweat suit in silence, ignoring the banter of his teammates. Then he stepped into the cool night air with his bag slung over his shoulder and a ball tucked under his arm.

And he started walking.

Reggie passed his bus stop and continued, heading north toward his neighborhood. As he walked, the anger simmered inside him. When he finally got home, Peggy was waiting.

"What's wrong?" she asked.

"Nothing, Mama," he answered. "I'm quitting basketball."

They sat at the kitchen table, and he told her the whole story. He talked about how unfairly he felt he was being treated. He said that he was sure he was better than some of the other players but that Coach Wade would never give him a chance to start. Peggy listened quietly. She never looked at her watch although she knew she would have to leave soon to get to her second job. (She was now working at a paper cup factory during the day and the tavern at night.)

"So why should I keep playing?" Reggie said.

"It's your decision, whether you quit or not," Peggy responded. "But if you ask me, you just can't stop because of this setback. You've put too much into this. It's too soon to give up now. If you really want to accomplish something, you have to be willing to keep working at it. If you are patient, success will come."

Reggie listened intently, and he took his mother's advice. He decided to stay on the team. Years later, after Reggie became a pro, he told Peggy, "Ma, you know, if it wasn't for you, I would have quit the game entirely back in high school. I was going to give it all up until you told me to give it another try."

Despite their perfect record by midwinter, the Poets were not even ranked number one in Baltimore. (That honor went to another unbeaten team.) Now came their most difficult test. They traveled to New Jersey to take on the number one high school team in the nation, the Camden Panthers. The Panthers were cocky, but the Poets weren't intimidated. Dunbar won so convincingly that all of the starters were on the bench well before the end of the game. Reggie got the playing time he craved. Among the Camden players who congratulated him afterward was Wes Fuller, who would become one of Reggie's close friends in college.

The Poets were on a roll. They won the Baltimore City Public Schools Tournament and then the State Championship. They finished the year with a perfect 28-0 record.

After the regular season, there was a high school all-star tournament in Baltimore. One of the eight teams scheduled to play backed out at the last minute, and Coach Wade was asked to put together a replacement squad of juniors and younger players. Several college scouts were at the tournament, including Karl Fogel, who was then assistant coach at Northeastern University. He was there to recruit a senior from one of Dunbar's rivals, Cardinal Gibbons High. It was another player who really caught his attention, though. "I noticed this tall, skinny kid dunking the ball all over the place and playing well," said Fogel.

"Who is that kid?" he later asked Coach Wade.

Wade said, "Reggie Lewis."

At Dunbar, varsity basketball players were celebrities. They signed autographs, they had a booster club, and they went on road trips that expanded their national prominence. When the players traveled, they stored their gear in a trunk, which became something of a trademark. "It was written once that we were like a traveling circus," Wade says. "What we did was bring pride to the community."

The girlfriends of team members also enjoyed a certain status in the school. "If you went with a varsity player, you were an item, you were popular," says Taresa. She had started dating Reggie long before he joined the team, however, and neither of them let all the attention go to their heads. They still enjoyed just relaxing together. "It was nothing for us to be at home watching TV all day long on a weekend," she says.

Taresa was looking forward to the Junior Prom. The whole idea of a formal dance was exciting to her — but not to Reggie.

"I don't want to go," he said.

"You're going," replied Taresa.

"No, I'm not. I don't want to," Reggie countered.

"Everybody is going!" she said.

"I don't want to go to any dumb prom," he said with a frown.

Taresa didn't give up easily. She argued, she coaxed, but he wouldn't budge. Finally, she offered a compromise.

"Tell you what. If you don't go to the Junior Prom, you are definitely going to the Senior Prom. No if's, and's, or but's about it, you understand?" she asked.

"I don't want to," he said emphatically.

"I'll let you off the hook this time, but you *are* going to the Senior Prom!" Taresa said as she looked him straight in the eye.

"All right," Reggie agreed.

Reggie knew how to dance — he and Taresa would go to clubs and parties occasionally — he just didn't like all the fuss associated with big social events. Given the choice, he would rather spend the evening at home. Sometimes he would urge Taresa to go alone. "You go ahead, it's all right," he would tell her. When the dance was over, she would stop by his house. "You look nice," he'd say.

Reggie may not have been a party type, but Taresa says he was attentive and romantic. On Valentines Day, he would give her a flower, some little stuffed animals, and a kiss. They also had a lot of fun together. Once Reggie stopped by Taresa's house on a day she was not supposed to have guests. Reggie, Taresa, and her cousin Kim were lounging around in Taresa's room when they got a glimpse through the window of Beverly walking toward the front steps. "Here comes your mother!" said Kim. They stuffed Reggie in the closet and closed the door. He didn't make a sound, so they forgot about him. Beverly finally left again to do some errands. Quite a while later, Kim asked, "Where's Truck?" She and Taresa looked at each other and said in unison:

"The closet!"

They opened the door.

"Girl!" Reggie said, frowning at Taresa.

He had been in there for two hours.

Reggie wasn't always on the receiving end. At her part-time job one day, Taresa became feverish and sick. She called Reggie. He told her to come to his house so he could look after her. By the time she got there, she was even more uncomfortable, and her temperature had gotten higher. Reggie decided he had to do something, so he took off her clothes, put her in the shower, and turned on the cold water full blast.

"Boy! What are you doing?" she shrieked.

"I thought that running cold water on you would break your fever," he said.

Never before had Reggie taken his school work so seriously. He was finally getting decent grades. The classes at Dunbar were challenging, and the teachers had a reputation for being evenhanded. "Some teachers resent athletes and give them a hard time for no reason," says Muggsy. "Sometimes it's the opposite — teachers cut athletes an unfair break, and then the other students resent them. At

Dunbar, though, the athletes were treated just like the other students. We had to do the work." Reggie and the rest of the players admired the school principal, Julia Woodland. She was friendly and supportive while keeping a tight rein on discipline: fights or suspensions almost never occurred.

Reggie rarely got upset. "His tolerance level was extremely high," says his aunt Dot. "He could take a lot." He was usually calm and happy. But there was an issue that was a sore spot for him.

As he glanced out a window at Dunbar one day, Reggie saw Taresa standing down below, talking to several of her friends. He smiled and was about to continue on his way when he did a double take: he noticed that the girls were passing something back and forth between them. They were smoking marijuana. Reggie bolted down the stairs and ran out the door to confront Taresa.

"What are you doing?" he yelled.

She was embarrassed at being discovered and surprised by Reggie's anger. She stood there, silently. Reggie grabbed her and shook her. "No girl friend of mine is going to be doing drugs! Promise me you won't ever do this again!"

Taresa nodded. "It was the only time he ever raised his voice at me," she says. She kept her pledge. She never again used pot.

Some time later, it became clear to Taresa why Reggie had reacted so strongly. They were at Reggie's house watching TV, and they took a break to get a snack. As they neared the kitchen, they smelled the telltale aroma of marijuana. They walked through the doorway and saw Peggy. She was sitting at the kitchen table, getting high.

"Please don't do that, Mama," he said.

"This is my house," she replied.

The scene was repeated several times. Each time Reggie became very upset. Once, he went up to his room and started crying. "He felt hurt," Taresa says. "He hated the fact that she was doing drugs. He could see the effect they had on her." As a result, Reggie became intensely opposed to drug use.

Taresa would comfort him. (She, too, had a relative who used drugs.) "Someday, Peggy will stop getting high," she would say. She would tell him that being upset about the situation would not do any good, and that instead, he should have hope. Reggie took the advice to heart. He never gave up on his mother.

Soon it was summer in the city. For Reggie, that meant Cecil-Kirk, city leagues, beach trips, crab feasts, and time to hang out with his friends and play a lot of basketball. Even when he went to visit Taresa, he often ended up in a game. Everyone in her neighborhood knew him, so when they learned he was around, guys would stop by and say, "Come on, Truck. Let's shoot some hoops." Taresa would sit on a swing and watch them play. Now and then, Reggie managed to coax her onto the court for a little one-on-one. After she had taken a few shots, he would smile and say, "Girl, we have to work on your jumper."

Reggie was invited to the Five Star basketball camp, which was held at a small college near Pittsburgh. The camp offered top college prospects a chance to show off their talent during the summer before their senior year. The players were assigned to different squads to compete in games.

Reggie put on an outstanding performance, eclipsing some more heralded players. Among the recruiters in the stands was Northeastern head coach Jim Calhoun. He agreed with his assistant coach's rave reviews. Reggie didn't look physically impressive — he was skinny and probably weighed no more than 160 pounds soaking wet — but he was surprisingly resilient and he could definitely shoot.

The family home was more crowded than usual that summer because Sheron had just given birth to a son, Joey, and Peggy was helping her care for the baby. Reggie and his brothers shared a bedroom on the front side of the house. There was a porch off Peggy's bedroom in the back where she would hang her wash.

Reggie and Taresa were walking around the corner to East Oliver Street one day when they spotted fire trucks parked down the block. Taresa and Reggie ran in that direction to see what had happened. In front of Reggie's house they stopped dead in their tracks. There was smoke curling from the upstairs windows; the painted trim was scorched black. The flames had been extinguished, but the second story of the row house was nearly gutted. It was around the Fourth of July, and some kids had carelessly tossed a lighted sparkler onto the porch. The sparks had ignited the clothes that were hanging there to dry.

Everything upstairs had been destroyed. The whole family was in tears as they poked through the soaked, charred remnants of what had been their clothing and cherished possessions. Reggie just shook his head as he looked around and thought of all they had lost. The fire meant moving again and starting over. With help from their relatives, however, Peggy and the children got back on their feet quickly.

It wasn't long before vacation was over and the Poets were preparing for their senior season. Despite the success of the previous year and a preseason number-one ranking by *Basketball Weekly*, Coach Wade was taking nothing for granted. The practices were as demanding and exhausting as ever. Reggie and his teammates responded, and they became closer than ever in the process. "We had a bond that has lasted forever," says Muggsy. "Even though we grew up and went our separate ways, we are still tied together."

Reggie seemed permanently tied to the role of sixth man, but his teammates thought no less of him for it. "We all knew he could play," says Reggie Williams. "He could drive the lane or hit the fifteen-foot jumper. He did a lot of things well." Muggsy adds: "On any other team in the country besides Dunbar, Reggie would have been The Man. And he was a huge part of our success. His not starting made no difference to us." But it did to Reggie.

Again, though, Reggie did not make his feelings known to Coach Wade. "He never complained about not starting," Wade says. "Whatever you asked him to do, he would respond in a positive manner." Wade liked being able to bring Reggie off the bench when the team needed a lift. "He could shoot from the perimeter and handle the ball like a guard," Wade says. "He gave us so much flexibility, and the tempo of the game picked up when he was in there."

College recruiters swarmed around Dunbar like bees to honey. Some of the starters signed early in the fall, but there wasn't a lot of interest in Reggie at first, except from

one school: Northeastern University. Reggie had never even
heard of the place. "I started asking my friends, 'You know
where this Northeastern is?' They all said, 'Nope,'" he
recalled.

Coach Calhoun made an appointment to meet Reggie and
his mother. Anthony Lewis and another coach from the
Cecil-Kirk center agreed to sit in. They helped prepare
Reggie with some tips on making a good impression. (Avoid
one-word answers; look people in the eye.)

When Calhoun arrived, he was led into the living room
of the house on North Rose Street. He looked around at the
people sitting there: the coaches, Irvin, Jon, Sheron, Peggy,
Taresa, and Reggie. "He was this skinny kid — about 6-5
— not saying a word but wearing this beautiful smile,"
Calhoun recalls.

Anthony told the coach, "You've been hearing about all
these great players we've got here, but this one is the best."

Reggie and his mother had a good feeling about Calhoun.
"He saw something in Reggie that no one else really had,"
Peggy says. Calhoun was sincere and animated as he
described the university, the basketball program, and the role
Reggie would play. And he used a word that was music to
Reggie's ears: "starter." He told Taresa that she might be
able to qualify for some financial aid if she wanted to come
to Northeastern with Reggie. Finally, Coach Calhoun invited
Reggie to fly up to Boston to visit the Northeastern campus.

Reggie made the trip, and he really liked the university.
"It was located in the city, which I wanted," he said. "It
was a great situation for me. It was a chance for me to get
away from home, but not too far. An hour plane ride. Plus,

they had a nice co-op program that I was really interested in. " Students at Northeastern are in a five-year program to allow for on-the-job training in their field of interest. When Reggie returned to Baltimore, he was excited. He was ready to make a verbal commitment to Northeastern.

The Poets' season was virtually flawless. They began by blowing away powerful DeMatha. At the highly-regarded King of Bluegrass Tournament in Kentucky, they crushed all their opponents. They racked up victory margins of over forty points in several of their regular season games. Reggie was still getting only limited playing time, but it was quality time, according to Coach Wade. One of the starters, Tim Dawson, tended to get in foul trouble, so Reggie was often playing at the final buzzer. Wade told his players, "It's not who starts, it's who finishes the game that's important. "

Over the Christmas holidays, Dunbar played in a tournament in Johnstown, Pennsylvania. The ground was blanketed with snow, and the wind was ripping through the trees with icy blasts. That wasn't enough to keep Jim Calhoun away, and quite a few other college coaches showed up, as well. Reggie had an excellent semifinal game to help the Poets advance to the championship round. In the finals, every one of Dunbar's starters got into foul trouble early. All except Muggsy eventually fouled out. For once, Reggie got playing time — lots of it. And he made the most of the opportunity. Dunbar won, and Reggie was named the Most Valuable Player of the tournament. "When I saw some of the things he could do," Calhoun says, "I started to get nervous." As Reggie was awarded the MVP trophy, Calhoun shifted in his seat and glanced at the other coaches in the stands. He was afraid they might try to steal Reggie out from under him.

Coach Wade and his wife had been invited out after the game, so he left his assistant in charge of supervising the players at the motel. Wade had a firm curfew rule, but this was a night for celebration. When Muggsy learned that the Coach would be away for a while, he said, "C'mon guys, let's leave here and go to a party."

Later that night, Coach Wade returned, and he noticed that the hallways were unusually quiet. He went to his assistant coach's room. Darryl Wood, who had sprained his ankle in the game, was there, and Reggie Williams, who never went out to party on the road. That was it. "Where is everybody?" Wade asked.

"Don't ask us," they said.

Wade started checking the other rooms. They were all empty. He finally got to Reggie's door and opened it. There was Reggie, sitting on his bed, eating donuts. Wade was surprised.

"You didn't go with everybody?"

"Nope."

"Why?"

"That's not my speed."

"Why not?"

"I played well tonight, Mr. Wade, and I was the Most Valuable Player. I'm not going out and messing up with you."

This kid has class, Wade thought.

Reggie saved his celebrating for his return home. He went to the bar where his mother worked to surprise her.

He walked in with his trophy. "It was almost as big as he was," Peggy remembers, "And the smile on his face!" Reggie held the trophy over his head.

"Look Ma! Look what I have for you!"

"Wow! Look at that! Oh, my goodness boy, what have you done!"

The Dunbar Poets were the top-ranked high school team in the nation throughout the season. They won the city championship for the seventh straight time and the state title for the sixth time in eight years. They went undefeated again: 31-0. That record, combined with the previous year's sweep meant the Poets had won 59 games in a row. It has been called the greatest high school team of all time. "I knew it was special at the time," says Coach Wade, "but not how special. Now, years later, I realize it probably was the best high school team ever assembled."

Wade says of all the players on that Dunbar team, Reggie showed the most improvement and made the most of his talents. "Whatever Reggie had to do to perfect his game," Wade says, "he would do. When he left Dunbar he had all the tools."

Late in the season, other colleges had begun "discovering" Reggie, as Jim Calhoun had feared. There were expressions of interest from Rutgers, Florida A&M, and George Washington, and more serious overtures from Penn State and Clemson. Then, at the last minute, Georgia Tech also made him an offer. Calhoun was worried, but Reggie never backed away from his original decision. He would honor his commitment to Northeastern. "He remembered we were there from the beginning," Calhoun said. "I've been coaching for two decades, and it's hard to find a kid who will stick to his convictions."

Reggie was starting to make some decisions not only about his college years but also about his life. He had toyed with the idea of joining the Marines if he had not received an athletic scholarship. Now that he was headed to Northeastern, he discussed the possibility of getting married and having children after graduating from college. As for a career choice, Taresa's mother, Beverly, gave him some advice. "Remember, you're not always going to play ball. Major in something that will profit you when you can no longer play." Reggie told her he had considered studying to be a dentist or dental technician. "Truck," Beverly responded, "get into something else." Whatever he ended up doing, Reggie knew he wanted to be in a position to help people.

Reggie's primary career goal involved basketball. For the first time ever, he set his sights on the NBA. He wasn't looking past college, but he now believed he could eventually have a professional playing career, given the right combination of hard work and good fortune.

Reggie told Taresa that if he ever made the pros, he was determined to do one thing in particular. "He was going to take care of his family, especially his mother," she says. "He loved his mother deeply and cherished her. He understood that because his mother was a single parent, she had a hard time raising him and his brothers and sister. He wanted to be able to buy her a house and a car. He promised me that he was going to take care of her for life so that she would never want for anything. He told me that many times. He felt strongly about it."

Reggie made good on his promise to take Taresa to the Senior Prom (although he balked at going to the Ring Dance —"That wasn't part of the deal," he said). During the week before graduation, Reggie was invited to go out to dinner with Taresa's family, including her mother, grandmother, and nephew Juan.

It was shrimp night at Duff's, a restaurant that featured an all-you-can-eat dinner buffet. Reggie and Juan were both big eaters. They returned from the serving line with plates piled high with food. They went back for seconds — and thirds — taking huge helpings each time. Beverly knew Reggie liked to eat, but she had never seen anything like this. Taresa's grandmother said, "They're embarrassing me." What the two ladies didn't know was that Taresa had brought along some plastic bags, and the boys were raking their food into them. Once back at home, Taresa revealed her stash: bags of shrimp, chicken, roast beef, baked fish, and dessert — everything except vegetables. There was enough for two day's worth of meals. The kids defended their scheme: "The sign said 'all you can eat.' It didn't say *when* you had to eat it."

Graduation Day arrived at last. The seniors were decked out in their maroon caps and gowns. After the procession and the speeches, an announcement was made of the students who had been awarded full college scholarships, including:

"Reggie Lewis, Northeastern University."

Until then, most of the people in the audience had not heard where Reggie was going. A huge cheer went up and resounded in the auditorium. It was a moment Peggy will never forget. She was beaming, and her heart was filled with pride.

To receive their diplomas, the seniors formed a single-file line that snaked past relatives gathered near the stage to snap pictures. When it was Reggie's turn and then Taresa's, their combined families screamed and made so much noise that people nearby pointed and chuckled. As he sat down, Reggie glanced at Taresa and whispered, "Are you humiliated enough? I wish they would be quiet."

Reggie's brother Irvin also graduated that day, from Patterson High School. Peggy and the family almost missed the ceremony because it followed Reggie's. Afterward, there was a big celebration at home. Most of the attention was focused on Reggie. Unlike his brother, he would be going to college on a basketball scholarship. But Reggie felt he still had something to prove.

Chapter Four

The Dream Team

Northeastern was a whole new world for Reggie — and a big one. He was one of over twenty thousand undergraduate students. The University was knit so well into the fabric of Boston's Back Bay area that it was hard to tell where the city ended and the campus began. Some of the old row houses in the neighborhood had even been converted into student living quarters. Getting anywhere in the city from campus was easy via Boston's rail transit system. It was an urban environment that felt familiar and comfortable to Reggie.

Peggy and Taresa flew with Reggie to Boston at University expense for freshman orientation. There was a special welcome for the new student-athletes. Their families were given a tour of the campus while the players met with Coach Calhoun and went out to dinner together.

Taresa had decided not to go to Northeastern, or any college, for a year. She was tired of school. She wanted to work and earn some money. And there was another reason. "We had been together for so long," she says. "By me staying in Baltimore, we would both have a chance to meet other people."

When it came time for Peggy and Taresa to leave Boston, there were lots of tears. Peggy told her son to do

his best, to study hard, and to enjoy himself. Taresa re-
minded him to call often. Reggie embraced each of them
and said goodbye. On the flight home, Taresa cried the
whole way.

Reggie returned to Matthews Arena and found his fellow
freshman recruits folding the tables used at orientation. He
pitched in and helped them clear off the court.

Then they played ball.

They didn't have to; they just wanted to. From that first
day, most of them would play nearly every day they were
students at Northeastern. They were Kevin Lee, Reggie's
roommate; Todd Granger; Wes Fuller, who had played
against Reggie in the game at Camden High; and Andre
LaFleur, Wes's roommate. Through basketball, this group
of first-year players established an immediate bond.

They decided to call themselves "The Dream Team."

The more they played, the more they sensed how their
personalities meshed. Reggie was the quiet one, of course,
but not quiet in a shy way. He now exuded a silent confidence. Kevin seemed like a project player who questioned
his own commitment to the game. Todd ended up leaving
Northeastern. Wes was the enforcer, the in-your-face type.
And Andre characterized himself as "the one who needed the
most support: the strength side from Wes and the good
playing side from Reg."

When Reggie was recruited, the coaches had no special
expectations for him. All of the freshmen they signed were
considered top notch players. Several days into the season,
however, Calhoun turned to one of his assistants during a
practice and said, "The skinny kid from Baltimore; he's a

little different." Reggie's teammates expected something special, too, especially as they got to know him better.

Several Dream Teamers were sitting around in a dorm room one day watching a game on TV. The University of Maryland's Len Bias drove toward the basket and dunked on an opposing team member, who shook his head in disgust. One of the players in the room said, "Gee, I don't know why that guy is so upset. When I was in high school, Bias used to dunk on me like that all the time."

Reggie looked at him with an expression of mild surprise. "If what you just said is true," Reggie remarked, "I don't know why you would tell anyone." There was silence in the room. Then Reggie asked, "Did you dunk on him back?" That's what he would have done.

Reggie finally achieved his dream of starting. From the beginning of the season, he and Andre were the only freshman starters. They quickly became very close friends because they both loved the game so much. At practice they would always be the first ones on the court. The coaches would look out their office window and see the two of them shooting around, laughing, and joking. They would also stay late after practice to continue refining their skills.

"Every time Reggie touched a basketball," Wes Fuller says, "he was working on his game. He wasn't just shooting to shoot, he was working on goals he had in his mind. That's how he developed his concentration."

A close circle of friendship developed among Wes, Andre, and Reggie. They were the core of the Dream Team, and they worked well together. Wes was a rebel. He didn't always agree with the coach, and he had no qualms about saying so. But he would listen to his pair of quieter pals.

Coach Calhoun once scheduled an extra practice, to begin at 10 p.m. Wes insisted that he wasn't going. He had studying to do. Enter Reggie and Andre.

"Now come on, Wes. If you don't go, he's going to dog you when you do come back."

Wes started to grumble.

"Just shut your darn mouth," they said, "and come on."

He did. Wes says that when Reggie and Andre told him to do something, "I might moan and groan and complain, but I did it anyway. We just could not disrespect each other, even when we didn't agree."

They learned a lot about leadership from the captain of the Huskies their freshman year, Mark Halsel. Mark set a good example. He practiced hard every day, and he was an excellent player. Like the coaches, he recognized the potential in Reggie. "Mark knew — although it was going to be his senior year — that Reggie was going to be the guy," says Coach Calhoun. "He kind of gave Reggie the mantle, to some degree, scoring-wise." Mark was like a big brother to the Dream Team. He was tough on them but fair, and he took time out to offer them advice and encouragement.

Much the same could be said for Calhoun. Under his guidance, Reggie flourished as a player. "From the first day we got there," Wes says, "Reggie was shooting and not missing." Reggie deeply appreciated the trust Calhoun placed in him by making him a starter, and he was determined to live up to that trust. When the Coach had a criticism or a suggestion, Reggie responded and tried harder. "He would run until his tongue fell out of his mouth," says his brother Jon, "and he would never complain — never." At Northeastern, Reggie concentrated on improving his game, not on proving himself.

Reggie seemed to know exactly what he needed to do to hone his skills. He became his own best coach. Early in the season, all of the players were told to go work out in the weight room. Reggie put in a brief appearance. "He picked up a couple of weights with his thin little arms," says Wes, "then he announced, 'All right. I've worked out. The heck with this, I'm out of here.' And he went and practiced his jump shot." That's how Reggie increased his strength and stamina: through intensive work on his game.

For the first few weeks he was at Northeastern, Reggie was homesick. He had never been away for more than a few days before, and he missed his family and Taresa. He called them frequently, sometimes more than once a day. Reggie remained proud of his Baltimore background. He wore his Poet's letter jacket his entire freshman year, even after his teammates started kidding him about it.

One day he got a call from Taresa that floored him.

"Guess what I did, Reggie."

"What?"

"I went and joined the Army."

"You did *what*?"

"I enlisted in the U.S. Army."

"Come on, you're joking!"

"No, it's true."

"Well, go get out of it! Tell them you've changed your mind."

"It's too late. I can't change it. I've already signed the papers."

Reggie was shocked and upset. He couldn't believe what she was saying. What about their plans together? He kept asking her why.

"I want to travel. I want to get away from home and grow up."

"But the *Army*? You're going to be a man!"

"No, I won't!"

They agreed to talk further and to stay in touch. Taresa told Reggie her feelings for him had not changed, but Reggie felt hurt by her decision. Taresa wrote to him and called while she was in basic training. For two or three months, Reggie didn't answer.

The Huskies spent a good deal of time on the road during the season. The team members would pass the time by playing cards for hours at a time — Tunk, Black Jack, and Pitty Pat. As always, Reggie cleaned up. "He was a card shark," says Wes. "Somehow he'd usually win."

Another favorite activity was wrestling. The Dream Team would take on their sophomore, junior, and senior teammates, pouncing on them in the hotel hallway or "kidnapping" them from their rooms. Even a couple of the assistant coaches got into the act. Occasionally, during all the jumping about and tussling, beds were broken. (Reggie felt right at home.)

On a trip to Buffalo to play Canisius, Coach Calhoun planned a visit to Niagara Falls. He made the excursion mandatory for the freshmen. Andre and Wes had no interest in seeing the Falls, but the Coach wasn't buying their excuses, so they enlisted Reggie in a scheme to get out of going. "Reggie, act like you're sick or something," Wes said, "and we'll tell the Coach we have to stay here with you."

By evening Reggie had made a remarkable "recovery," and Andre and Wes persuaded him to go out, despite the Coach's request that the team stay in. Later that night when they returned, Reggie, Andre, and Wes stepped into the hotel elevator, only to find Coach Calhoun inside. Reggie, of all people, spoke up to break the silence. "Hey Coach, what's up? How are you doing?" Wes and Andre couldn't believe their ears. Reggie continued, "All right Coach, see you tomorrow. Have a good night's sleep." By the time the elevator door opened, everyone — including the Coach — was laughing.

Reggie and Andre shared a passion for basketball. They enjoyed everything about the game, not just playing it. If one of them had some money, they would split it and spend every dollar on basketball posters and gear — especially shoes. "We were fanatical about sneakers," Andre says. "We had to have the latest and the best."

They went to sports pubs so they could watch three games at once on big screen TV's. Although they rarely talked about their own games, they sat and discussed basketball strategy. They hopped the trolley and went to see other college teams and occasionally even a high school contest. And whenever they had enough cash, they would go to a Celtics home game at the Boston Garden.

Both Reggie and Andre were fans of the Los Angeles Lakers, and in particular, Magic Johnson. (Reggie also liked the Iceman, George Gervin of the San Antonio Spurs.) "Every time we went to the Garden," Andre says, "we would be about the only people in the stands rooting against the Celtics." At a play-off game they attended, they sat in the front row, gloating when Boston was on the brink of defeat. But the Celtics pulled out a victory, and the fans celebrated by pelting Reggie and Andre with cups and other debris. "We hated the Celtics," Andre says.

Reggie and Andre also had something else in common: a yen for oriental martial arts movies. Every Sunday, they would take the trolley to Chinatown and spend the day watching four or five karate and kung fu films at a theater there. In fact, they liked all kinds of movies, and they made a point of seeing new releases as soon as they came out.

When Reggie went home for Christmas vacation, Peggy welcomed him with his favorite meal: fried chicken, collard greens, rice, and potato salad. As he ate, he talked about how well the team was doing and about how much he liked Northeastern. "He was doing something he really loved," Peggy says, "and he was finally getting recognition. He appreciated all the attention he was getting."

Taresa was home for Christmas, too. She went to see Reggie, hoping to sort things out, but she found that he was acting differently toward her. "Let's see how many pushups you can do," he said. He challenged her to a pushup competition and a race.

"I guess he thought that because I joined the Army, I wasn't feminine anymore," Taresa says. "I assured him I was the same woman I had always been." Reggie was skeptical. Her uniform bothered him. She could sense that they were growing apart.

Taresa was stationed in West Point, N.Y., not too far from Boston. When Reggie became aware that she was dating other men, he started to call her. Several times, he asked her to come visit him at Northeastern. He said he would even pay for her plane ticket. She never made the trip.

Reggie had an outstanding freshman season, averaging 17.8 points and 6.2 rebounds. He was named ECAC North Atlantic Conference Rookie of the Year. The Huskies finished 27-5, their best record ever. They won the conference title and a bid to the NCAA tournament. There, they suffered a one-point loss at the buzzer to Virginia Commonwealth, but Reggie was superb, shooting 15 for 17 from the floor.

Coach Calhoun admitted he was surprised by Reggie's rapid rise to prominence. "I thought with time he could be a good power forward," he said at the time, "but his development has been tremendous." The Coach was even more impressed with Reggie as a person. "The thing that stands out is that he's just a good human being," Calhoun said. "He's a really humble kid. We're a work-oriented school, and Reggie's a real worker."

Reggie didn't stop working on his game just because the season had ended. Most of the other members of the team took a break, but Reggie and Andre kept playing nearly every day.

"We could play one-on-one for hours," Andre says. On weekends, for variety, they would go to Harvard, Boston College, and other universities in the area. "The coaches would open up the gyms and let us play," Andre says.

"Sometimes we would be the only ones there." They were often joined on these outings by another first year student, Mark Reeves, who was not a member of the team. He became one of Reggie's closest friends.

Wes was not around as much now because he had joined a fraternity, Iota Phi Theta, which was popular with basketball team members. Reggie, Andre, and Mark were always welcome at the fraternity's functions, but they decided not to join. "We just didn't see the point," Mark says. "We knew we could be popular and enjoy ourselves without belonging to a frat. We wanted to be different." At one point, they even considered starting a social club of their own. Instead, they often hung out at the Punter's Pub on campus, although the crowd there was made up mainly of football and hockey players. They became such regulars that the manager added pictures of Reggie and Andre to the collection of athletic photos on the wall. The bartenders even slipped them free drinks now and then.

Although basketball was Reggie's main interest at Northeastern, he kept up with his studies. He went to class, did his homework, and got average grades. "He was no dummy," says Wes. "He didn't take easy courses." When his teammates were in a pinch, he offered to type their papers for them. At the start of his sophomore year, Reggie decided to major in criminal justice to prepare himself for an eventual career in working with young people.

Some people assumed that Reggie's friendly, low-key manner meant he would be a pushover on the basketball court. That was a mistake. "He had an inner strength that most never saw," says Coach Calhoun.

Andre was on his way to class one day when he spotted Reggie playing one-on-one against another member of the team. "This guy," he says, "was the best one-on-one player on the team. He was tough, he worked out with weights, and he had huge hands, like Doctor J."

The game became heated very quickly. Reggie was being fouled and wasn't calling them. His opponent, however, was angrily calling anything close to an infraction by Reggie.

"Foul! Give me the ball!" he said.

Reggie handed it to him and went on defense. His opponent drove in for a layup, and Reggie blocked it cleanly. "They faced off, and the guy shoved Reggie, who was much thinner than he was," Andre says. "I was thinking, 'Oh no, Reg is in trouble now.' But Reggie shoved him back, then squared his feet and put his hands up like a boxer. The other guy was surprised and hesitated." During that pause, Andre stepped in and defused the situation. He had learned something about his friend, though. Reggie was a lot tougher than he seemed.

Reggie never called fouls in pickup games or one-on-one. Even if he was hacked several times and missed a shot as a result, he would not protest. He didn't talk trash or complain. He just kept going to the basket.

About the only person Reggie would needle on the court was Andre. Their marathon one-on-one games were a study in different styles of winning and losing. The ritual was always the same. They would put their gear on opposite sides of the gym. As the game began, they would be telling each other, "Aw man, you can't play!" Andre used certain advantages to compensate for Reggie's superior ability. "I would always call fouls, and he never would," Andre says. "We only played to seven, and we had a three-dribble rule which made it so he couldn't back me in. We played a perimeter game. If I hit a couple of jumpers and went to the basket a few times, I had a chance." Sometimes Reggie would sweep the games; sometimes Andre would. The loser would always gather his belongings and leave the gym in a funk.

When Andre won, he would gloat. "Yes! Yes!" he would shout, "I kicked your butt again! You couldn't stop me!" He would continue the taunting all the way across campus, trying to get under Reggie's skin. Reggie hated that, but he usually managed to keep his cool.

When Reggie won, he would gently tease his friend. Andre would mumble that he was going home as he stormed out of the gym, but Reggie would follow, talking to him quietly all the way.

"So, you're mad now, huh? Aren't you my friend anymore? Let's go back to the gym. I'll let you win the next game."

Andre would pick up the pace, but Reggie would keep up with him and continue his monologue.

"Remember that shot I blocked that was game point and you wanted a foul? All right, I'll give you that foul, so that was a game. That means you won one game today. Are you happy now?"

Eventually, no matter who had won, they would both see the humor in the situation, start chuckling, and head out to get some pizza. "We were very competitive, but in a friendly way," Andre says. There were never any lingering hard feelings.

"Reg and Andre would love to argue about nothing — absolutely nothing — just for the sake of arguing," says Wes. "It was always playful, however. Reggie liked to get you upset then sit back with his little gremlin face and laugh."

For security, the dorm where Reggie lived had a proctor stationed at the door to check ID's. One day when Reggie was returning to his room, he noticed an attractive young woman sitting at the desk. Reggie was curious. He asked some of his friends in the dorm about her. She was a student from Bridgeport, Connecticut, he found out, and her name was Donna Harris. Reggie was finally introduced to Donna at a party they attended. "They got on the dance floor," Andre recalls, "and I don't think they ever stopped dancing."

Reggie was assigned to a different dorm for his sophomore year. He and Andre each had single rooms, but they roomed together when the team went on the road. Coach Calhoun gave the players a lot of leeway when they traveled. They never had specific curfews. The only rule was that they had to be ready to play well at game time.

The night before a game in Vermont, Reggie, Wes, and Andre visited the campus and went to a late party. It was snowing heavily, and the ground was blanketed by the time they got back to the motel where the team was staying. "We were laughing and having a good time," Andre says. "We knew where the coaches' room was, so we all made snowballs and pelted the door. Then we ran to our rooms." The next morning, there was not a word about the "attack" from the coaches. "They knew it was us," Andre says, "but they would wait. If we lost, we would be in trouble. If we won, there would be no problem." They did win the game, easily. Later, Coach Fogel had a smile on his face when he took Andre aside.

"By the way, I heard you and the others throwing those snowballs."

"What are you talking about? How do you know I was involved?"

"Andre, they were all shouting your name."

Hanging out on the eve of road games became something of a tradition, but Reggie wouldn't always go along. He liked to rest before big games.

"Reg, are you ready, man? We're going," Wes and Andre would say.

"No, I'm tired. I'm staying in."

"Do you want us to bring you back something to eat?"

"Yeah, bring me a cheeseburger."

By the time they got back, however, Reggie would usually be asleep.

The Huskies were in the midst of another excellent season when they went to Providence to play in a Christmas tournament. It was almost exactly three years after Reggie's standout performance coming off the bench for Dunbar in the Johnstown tournament. The Huskies stumbled in the opening round, and they lost again in the consolation game. But Reggie's exceptional playing earned him the Most Valuable Player award. "It was then that I knew Reggie would be a pro," Wes says. "The coaches, the people — they just loved him."

Northeastern repeated as North Atlantic Conference champions. In the title-clinching showdown with Boston University, Reggie scored 29 points, despite breaking his wrist early in the game. The Huskies went 22-9 for the year. Reggie earned All-East honors and was named the NAC Player of the Year. He was also the top collegiate sophomore scorer in the nation, with a 24.1 points-per-game average.

Although he didn't look as imposing physically as some other players, Reggie was talented and disciplined, and he understood the game well. "He knew how to use his body to its best advantage," Andre says. "He had a lot of skills. He could shoot and score, of course, but could also play defense, grab rebounds, and block shots. He had a kind of wiry strength and just a good sense of the game."

Reggie was becoming closer to Donna. She was the sweetheart of the Iota fraternity, and she understood the life of a basketball player. In some ways, Donna and Reggie were opposites: while he was easygoing, private, and quiet, she was gregarious, outspoken, and shoot-from-the-hip direct. "I think the relationship helped Reggie during our college years," Wes says. "He seemed to gain more confidence in himself, and he became more outgoing."

Andre agrees. "Donna belonged to a sorority, and she had clout around campus," he says. "She was a social person with lots of friends, and she kind of brought out Reggie's social side."

When Donna moved to an apartment just across Huntington Avenue from campus, Reggie began spending a good deal of time there. The building, which was located next to a pizza shop, was old and rundown, but Donna kept the apartment neat. She shared the place with a roommate who had a one-year-old son. As for the decor, there were wooden floors, a few pieces of furniture, and bookshelves made of crates. "It looked like a dorm room," says Stacy Quarterman, who lived next door. Reggie would come to study, and Donna would fix a meal for them. Sometimes they invited Stacy over to share the food. "Donna was a good cook," Stacy says. Once, Stacy gave Reggie a birthday cake with a "35" (his jersey number) on the icing. "He was surprised and very appreciative," she says.

Reggie and Taresa talked several times over the summer. Taresa had decided she wanted to start seeing him again, but it was too late. Reggie told her he really liked Donna. "He kept calling for a while," Taresa says, "then he stopped." They remained good friends, however, and she sometimes visited Reggie when he came back to Baltimore to see his family.

At the start of their junior year season, Reggie, Andre, and Wes were named co-captains of the team. The Huskies picked right up where they left off. They defeated most of their opponents until they took to the road to play one of their conference arch-rivals: Siena College. Northeastern lost that game before a packed house of venomous Siena fans, in part because Reggie had an unusually bad day. Afterward, the Siena player who had guarded him bragged about shutting Reggie down, and he implied that he would do it again during the rematch at Northeastern.

Whenever Reggie felt he had been personally challenged, he rose to the occasion, and he responded with actions, not words. In this case, he had a simple plan. "I just wanted to come out and 'spree' my points on him and prove that I was a better player than he was," he recalled. A sellout crowd at Matthews Arena saw him do just that. During the return match with Siena, Reggie scored 41 points, a career high, and the Huskies got their revenge.

Northeastern again won the North Atlantic Conference crown, with a 26-5 record. Reggie repeated as conference Player of the Year. He averaged 23.8 points per game and 9.3 rebounds. In the NCAA tournament, the Huskies put up a strong challenge to highly-favored Oklahoma before losing. Reggie scored 35 points in the game.

By now, Reggie and his buddies all had girlfriends (Andre was engaged). Reggie had moved in with Donna. When he gave up his dorm room, he started receiving several hundred dollars a semester from the University to help defray the cost of off-campus housing. The money didn't go far, though. Donna was working a part-time job to help cover the bills. About all Reggie and Andre could afford when they went out for snacks were fifty-cent plain slices at one of the nearby pizza joints.

Reggie and his teammates had all the ingredients for a great senior season, but they had to deal with one major change. Jim Calhoun had departed for another coaching job. Assistant Coach Fogel was named as his replacement. He had big shoes to fill. The players loved Calhoun, and some of them believed Fogel was too eager to tinker with the Huskies' successful formula. "Sometimes in your senior year," Wes says, "you can't really coach players, you have to just let them play what they feel." Under Fogel's direction, however, the Huskies continued their winning ways.

A favorite weekend excursion for Reggie, Andre, and Mark was to drive down to Cape Cod for a day of fishing and relaxing. Mark's parents had a house and a boat there. Mark had graduated early, but he still went to see the Huskies when they played at home.

Before one game, Mark had a proposition for Reggie. "If you get 28 points tonight," he said, "we'll go down to the Cape, and I'll pay for everything." Northeastern was playing Vermont, not exactly heavy lifting for the Huskies, who rolled to a commanding lead. With two minutes left, however, Reggie only had 27 points. Then he was fouled. As he went to the free throw line, Reggie gazed up into the stands until he spotted Mark. He put the first shot up — swoosh! Reggie again glanced at Mark. Second shot — swoosh! "Even with the game out of reach," Mark says, "he still had a point to prove."

After the game, Reggie strolled up to his friend and said, "Twenty-nine. I'll be ready to leave in a second."

Reggie liked to shine in competition, but he never did so at the expense of his teammates. When the Huskies played at the University of New Hampshire, Reggie was set to break the Northeastern record for consecutive games in double figures. He got into foul trouble early in the second half, and Coach Fogel pulled him out for a rest. While Reggie was on the bench, the team scored a flurry of points. Reggie only had nine, so the Coach asked him if he wanted to go back in and break the record. No, Reggie said, he was enjoying watching the reserves run up the score. He told Fogel, "Let those guys have fun and play."

After a hard practice one day, Andre and Reggie got a bite to eat and hung out for a while. They were tired, though, so they decided to call it an evening. Andre went home and switched on his TV. He had been there only about half an hour when the telephone rang.

"'Dre, man, I burned my hand." It was Reggie.

"Yeah, right! Quit playing on the phone." Andre thought he was joking.

"No, I'm serious, I burned it. Man, I need you to come over."

"Right. I just took my shoes off, and I'm beat. I'm not coming over there."

Andre hung up the phone.

But as he sat watching TV, his mind kept drifting back to the call. Reggie never complained about anything, he thought. He could play right through injuries. Something wasn't right. Andre put his sneakers back on and jogged over to Reggie's apartment.

Reggie opened the door. He was standing there cradling his right hand in his left.

"Look," he said.

"Man, what did you do?"

All the skin on part of his hand was peeled back, even off the fingers. "You could even smell the burned skin," Andre says. "It was terrible."

Reggie explained what had happened. He was cooking french fries (something he loved), and had the oil heating on the stove. He covered the pot with a top that had just been washed and still had some water around the rim. When he lifted the top, drops of water fell into the pot, causing the hot oil to flare up and spatter. In a split-second, his hand was badly burned.

"We've got to go to the hospital," Andre said.

Donna was at work, so Reggie and Andre pooled what little money they had — about four dollars between them — and took a cab to University Hospital.

The doctors who examined the hand told Reggie the burn was serious. They said he would have to remain in the hospital at least overnight. The dead skin was removed, and the wound was bandaged. By now Reggie's hand was swelling badly. If there wasn't some improvement by the next day, he was told, the doctors would have to make an incision to relieve the pressure. Andre called Donna and Coach Fogel to give them the news. "The injury had to be painful," Andre says, "but as usual, Reggie didn't complain."

The swelling went down on its own, but Reggie stayed in the hospital for a couple of days to rest. Andre brought him magazines to help pass the time. The hospital was supposed to be screening visitors to keep the press away, but one photographer managed to slip in under the guise of being a friend. He was apologetic when he entered the room, but he begged for permission to shoot a couple of pictures. Reggie finally agreed. The photo of Reggie and his bandaged hand ran in the *Boston Globe* sports section the next day.

The injury kept Reggie out of a few games, but his misfortune turned out to be a break for Andre, who stepped in to help fill the scoring gap. "Until then," Andre says, "I was just known as the guy who passed the ball to Reggie." Andre was the point guard for the Huskies, and he broke the NCAA record for assists. "I always joked with Reg that I was the one who made his career, so he was forever in debt to me," Andre says. "But by senior year, Reggie was telling me, 'If it wasn't for me, you wouldn't have broken that record and set yourself up for the draft.'"

The NBA draft also loomed large in Reggie's future. He had visited the Boston Celtics rookie training camp, and he came away convinced that he had what it took to be a professional. "I had a chance to play with some of the pros at the camp," he said, "and I held my own. I really felt I'd have a chance."

Reggie was not phoning home as frequently as he once did anymore, but when he did call, he began to notice a change in his mother. She seemed detached somehow, and their conversations were shorter and more superficial. "I was there but I really wasn't there," Peggy says. "I wasn't fully focused when he called." There was a reason.

When he was home for a weekend around Mother's Day, Reggie strolled into Peggy's room along with Irvin to ask her something. He was shocked by what he saw. On her bed was a large pile of marijuana that she was portioning into small plastic bags. Reggie and Irvin circled the bed, watching her. Finally, Reggie broke the silence.

"Ma, are you *selling* this stuff?"

"Yes, I am," she admitted.

Reggie didn't say another word. He didn't have to. "This look came on his face," Peggy recalls. "I'll never forget it. He looked deeply disappointed in me. When I saw his expression, I felt so embarrassed."

Reggie stared at the floor as he walked out of Peggy's room. There was little he could do, he decided, except pray for his mother and hold out hope that she would find the

strength to kick her habit. What he didn't know at the time
was that Peggy's drug habit was no longer limited to marijuana. She had also begun to dabble in cocaine.

Reggie, Wes, and Andre savored their senior season at
Northeastern. "Every game was different — and special,"
Wes says. "We helped each other out and made each other
better. We had good times together." Their road trips
included a journey to Alaska to appear in the Great Alaska
Shootout. "It was like no place we had ever seen in our
lives," recalls Wes. They upset Louisville before losing to
Iowa in the finals. In the team's last game of the season, at
the NCAA tournament, Reggie put on a display of long-
range shooting, scoring 23 points in a valiant, losing effort
against Purdue. He always seemed to have his best games
when the competition was toughest.

The Huskies won their fourth straight North Atlantic
Conference championship. Their final record was 27-7.
Reggie earned his third consecutive conference Player of the
Year award, after leading the team with an average of 23.3
points per game. He also shattered some significant records.
He became Northeastern's all-time leading scorer with 2,709
points, and he was the ninth leading scorer in the history of
the NCAA.

Although Reggie was one of the nation's top collegiate
players, his accomplishments did not draw much notice
outside of New England because Northeastern was not
considered a basketball power. By contrast, his former
Dunbar teammates David Wingate and Reggie Williams
received widespread attention as members of Georgetown
University's national championship team, and Muggsy

Bogues was acclaimed for breaking Atlantic Coast Conference records at Wake Forest. Yet Reggie never had any regrets about going to Northeastern. "If I had gone to another school, I might not have had the chances I had here," he said. "This has been a great place for me."

When the season was over, Reggie was invited to play in the Aloha Classic in Hawaii, a tournament for likely first-round draft picks. Despite a splendid showing, he didn't even make the tournament all-star team. "I don't know why," he said later. "I averaged something like 20 points and 12 rebounds a game. I should have been the MVP of the whole tournament."

Reggie was a star, but he was a hidden star: he had not yet gotten all the recognition he deserved. He wasn't discouraged; he just became more determined to improve his skills further and to take his game to the next level of competition.

Chapter Five

Respect

The pain in his ankle caused Reggie to wince. He tried to walk it off, hobbling at first. Later, he was able to continue playing, but he was not at full speed. Up in the stands, one of the scouts wrote "tough break" in his notebook under Reggie's name. The event was a pre-draft tryout camp in Chicago.

Other prospective pros might have been dejected after such an ill-timed injury, but not Reggie. He didn't let it bother him, and he didn't dwell on it. In describing the camp to his friend Mark, Reggie said: "I had to guard this guy, Pippen. He was pretty good, but you know, my ankle was messed up. He's a pretty good ball player." Then again, Reggie called everyone a good ballplayer. "Even me," says Mark. "He gave people a lot of credit." Some of the scouts weren't so generous. They downgraded Reggie after his disappointing performance at the camp.

Coach Fogel spoke to several scouts to try to dispel their doubts. He told them Reggie had a quicker first step than anyone except Michael Jordan. "But people questioned how he would stand up physically," Fogel said. A scout from Atlanta said his organization simply felt Reggie couldn't play.

A few of Reggie's acquaintances suggested that he prepare for the possibility that he might not be drafted in the first round. Reggie wasn't worried. "I was sure I would be drafted," he said, "even if nobody else was." He didn't allow his expectations to become overly-inflated, though. "He thought he was good enough to make it in the NBA," Mark says, "but he also felt he would be fortunate if he made it — like hitting the lottery."

On draft day, Reggie and Donna sat on the bed of their small studio apartment and turned on the TV to watch the selections being announced. They were joined by Mark and one of Donna's friends. Reggie had been projected to go around 15th or 16th, but that was before the tryout camp. Everyone leaned forward as the mid-round picks were made: 15, 16, 17 . . . still no Reggie . . . 19, 20, 21. The next selection belonged to the Boston Celtics, but Reggie was sure they weren't interested. They had not contacted him or said they were considering choosing him. They were likely to take a center from the University of Houston, he thought.

What Reggie didn't know was that the Celtics' Rick Weitzman, a Northeastern graduate, had spent considerable time scouting him and watching him develop as a player. Reggie's poor tryout camp showing didn't worry the Celtics. General manager Jan Volk said, "We knew too much about him to change our opinion because of a few bad days."

The 22nd pick was about to be announced. The first round would soon be over. Just then, the telephone in the apartment rang, and Reggie answered it. A look of surprise lit up his face. Before anyone could ask what had happened, the image of Celtics president Red Auerbach appeared on the TV screen.

"The Boston Celtics select Reggie Lewis from Northeastern."

Reggie took a deep breath. He sat up straight for a moment on the edge of the bed, then he fell backward onto the mattress with his arms outstretched. He was grinning from ear to ear.

Two of Reggie's Dunbar teammates were also first round picks: Reggie Williams was taken by the Clippers and Muggsy Bogues by the Bullets. It was the first time three players from the same high school had ever been selected during the first round of the draft in the same year. "I never dreamed it would work out like this," Reggie said as reporters started to call. During their years at Dunbar, the three players had talked about the possibility of playing together in the NBA, but they never really thought that it would happen.

Reggie changed into the pinstripe suit he had chosen for the occasion, then he hopped the trolley to the Boston Garden. The reporters who were there to monitor the draft gathered around to ask for his reaction. "This is great," he said. "I was hoping I'd go to the Celtics; I was ready to go anywhere. They have a lot of talent. I think I'll be playing off guard, but when anybody needs a break, I'll be ready to go in." For his first news conference as a pro, Reggie said all the right things.

Back at the apartment, Reggie phoned his mother at work. "Mama, I was drafted by the Boston Celtics!" he said.

"You were? Get out of here!" she replied. Then she added, "Who are they?" Peggy was never much of a basketball fan, but she could hear the excitement in Reggie's voice, and she felt proud and happy for him.

Andre was happy for both Reggie and himself. (He had been drafted in the later rounds.) Just the thought of Reggie being chosen by the team they had rooted against had him chuckling. Later that day, they finally had a chance to talk.

"The *Celtics*?" Andre said. They both laughed loudly. "And what's this stuff about always being for the Celtics?" he added.

"Hey man, that's my team now." Reggie answered, turning more serious.

Andre thought for a moment, then nodded. "You're right; you're right. Good team."

That day, Reggie and his friends all became instant Celtics fans.

For all their glowing statements about Reggie on draft day, the Celtics hedged their bet by signing him to a one-year contract at the NBA salary minimum (around $75,000 that year). That was still more money than Reggie had ever seen. He began sending checks to his mother to help her out, and he bought a few things for himself. There was one purchase in particular that he called home to tell Peggy about.

"Ma, remember that blue bike I once had? I got myself a brand new bike today."

Reggie also got himself a new place to live: a rented condominium in Dorchester at Harbor Point. The development offered to sponsor him if he would hold basketball clinics for them. He had the home to himself for a while. Donna moved out.

Although Reggie and Donna were engaged, they agreed they needed some time living apart. Donna moved into an apartment of her own for several months. She got a job and paid her own bills. Reggie and Donna continued seeing each other during this period, and, if anything, the separation seemed to strengthen their relationship. "This was a good time for them," Andre says, "because it really proved that Donna could be independent. She gave him space and had her own life, until they were married. Reggie appreciated that."

During his rookie year, Reggie felt unappreciated by the Celtics. He found himself in an all-too-familiar place most of the time: on the bench. Reggie averaged fewer than five points and less than ten minutes of playing time per game. Celtics coach K.C. Jones was following a team tradition that he himself had experienced. Rookies were expected to watch and wait their turns, but it made no sense to Reggie. "I'm killing them in practice," he would tell Mark, so he didn't understand why he was not getting more playing time.

Reggie's frustration was heightened when fans started pestering him about the situation. People would come up to his table when he was out to dinner with Donna and urge him to criticize the coach publicly. Reggie would turn to Donna and say quietly, "Don't worry. It won't always be like this." Fans would flock around him on the street and ask why the Celtics weren't using him. He had no answer. It was the same question he was asking himself.

When Andre spoke to Reggie, he tried to boost his spirits. "You are destined to be a pro; you've just got to pay your dues," he said.

"It's going to be all right," Reggie replied, halfheartedly. Then Andre related a conversation he'd had with his dad, who was a longtime Celtics fan. His father's theory was that the Celtics really liked Reggie but that they were "hiding" him because he was on a one-year contract. If they let him show his skills, they would either lose him to another team or have to spend a bundle to re-sign him. Whether the explanation was true or not, Reggie felt better after hearing it.

Even more helpful was the support he was getting from Celtics veterans who were impressed by the fact that he never complained about his limited role. "That was Reggie," said Dennis Johnson. "Even when times were hard for him, he was cruising. Nothing bothered him because he wouldn't let it bother him."

Dennis, Danny Ainge and Larry Bird all gave Reggie some simple advice that he said helped him a great deal: "Have patience, work hard, and your time will come."

The wait seemed endless. During one three-and-a-half month stretch late in the season, Reggie never played a single minute while any game was up for grabs, although the Celtics' starters were fading. Finally, toward the end of the play-off series with Atlanta, Coach Jones had nowhere else to turn. Reggie got the call.

He responded with two excellent games that offered fans a taste of things to come. "Sometimes, as soon as he got in, he would go to the hoop, catching defenders off guard," Andre recalls. "He was confident, but he didn't dare his opponents. For Reggie it was just, 'If you give me the ball, I'll take you to the hole.' The Celtics re-signed Reggie and boosted his pay into six figures.

In the off-season, it was just like old times in Baltimore when Reggie went home for visits. The family would gather at Peggy's, and Reggie would join them for an evening of playing cards and eating hardshell crabs. He missed Eastern Shore crabs so much that he would freeze some and take them back to Boston with him. When he ran out, Peggy would ship him crab meat packed in dry ice.

Most of the money Reggie sent his mother for household expenses each month was being used to support what was now her addiction to cocaine. Rather than continuing to pay Peggy directly, Reggie decided to help his mother buy a house, a modest duplex where she still lives. He did the same for his sister Sheron. Reggie covered the monthly mortgage payments for both homes.

Reggie's patience paid off in his second year as a pro. Gone was the coach who had confined him to the bench. When Larry Bird sustained an injury that required season-ending surgery only six games into the Celtics' schedule, the new coach, Jimmy Rodgers, chose Reggie to fill the scoring void. Reggie became a starter, a position he held from then on.

Once he had the chance to play, Reggie delivered. He led the team in steals, and he averaged over 18 points a game, even more in the play-offs. In five games he scored over 30 points, including one 39-point performance against Philadelphia. He was also the runner-up in the balloting for the Most Improved Player in the NBA. Reggie was grateful for that distinction, but he didn't really think it was accurate. The improvement was more in his playing time than in his ability.

"In Reggie's mind, he was always there," Mark says. "He felt he was doing the same things in games that second year that he had been doing in practice his rookie year."

Dennis Johnson agreed. "What Reggie was doing out there a lot of people found a surprise, but not the players on the team. There was excitement waiting to jump out every time he walked onto the court."

As a starter, Reggie played with greater ease. "[Rookie] year, I got too pumped up when I got in the game and put pressure on myself," he said. "It was like when I was in high school. Replacing Larry as the starting forward gave me the opportunity to make mistakes and not worry about trying to do everything at once to impress the coach. I could relax and play my game."

One contest in particular represented a kind of coming of age for Reggie as a pro. On December 6, 1989, the Celtics played the Chicago Bulls. Reggie was matched against Michael Jordan, and he totally outperformed the superstar, scoring 33 points with four assists and six rebounds.

Reggie quickly became a favorite of Boston fans, but there was a downside to his new popularity. People were constantly asking him for autographs, which he didn't mind, but some seemed intent on hassling him simply because he was a celebrity. When he was out in public, Reggie often relied on Mark to help insulate him from troublemakers and loudmouths. Some places offered a more hospitable atmosphere than others. Reggie liked to return to the area around Northeastern because people there were so used to seeing him that they took his presence in stride.

If Reggie was driving through a tough neighborhood and teenagers shouted out his name, he would pull over to greet them. Some people warned him this wasn't a good idea because he might get robbed. Reggie shrugged off the advice, though. "If I *don't* stop, and they see me again, they might rob me," he said. He always wanted to be known as a person who cared.

Reggie never flaunted his fame, but he was eager for his family to share in his success, and he was very generous. He took his mother and his father shopping and told them to buy whatever they wanted. He arranged a back-to-school shopping spree for his nieces, nephews and cousins in Baltimore — more than a dozen children in all. It took a caravan of cars to transport them to the mall.

On one of Jon's visits to Boston, Reggie picked up his brother at the train station. Outside, walking to Reggie's Jeep, they were "ambushed" by a posse of pint-sized fans with squirt guns. Reggie dodged the dousing after a few moments, and ran into a nearby store to buy a newspaper. When he came out, he carried something else, as well. "Reggie had noticed that two of the children didn't have water pistols," Jon says, "so he bought each of them one." The two boys filled their gifts up quickly so they could join their buddies in a farewell squirting attack. A soaked Reggie finally scrambled to shelter in the Jeep with Jon, and they drove off, laughing.

Mark and Reggie spent a lot of time together during the summer months. They liked to shoot pool, take road trips to Baltimore and Washington, and go fishing at Cape Cod. "Seldom did we plan ahead," Mark says. "We would get up

early and spend the day on the boat, trolling for bluefish."
Mark's dad never treated Reggie like a star. Instead, he
would order him to cast off ropes and to do other tasks on
the boat. Reggie enjoyed being just another member of the
"crew."

With the return of Larry Bird, Reggie was asked to carry
less of the offensive load during his third season. He
continued to start, but he was forced to split his time
between small forward (Bird's position) and guard. Adding
to the uncertainty, the guard rotation was in flux. "It was
confusing in the beginning," Reggie said. "We didn't know
who was going to be out there or when." As a result,
Reggie's scoring average edged down. During the last ten
games of the regular season, however, when some of his
teammates were sagging, he boosted his output to 23.5 points
per game.

One of Reggie's strengths was his versatility. "If you
defend against him real well," said then-assistant coach Chris
Ford, "he can still beat you with the dribble. He can create,
get open or take it to the basket, and we don't have any other
player who can do that."

There was some grumbling during the season about
Bird's role on the team. Fans were telling Reggie that he
now deserved to own the small forward spot because he was
better than Bird. Reggie wanted to hear straight talk, not
hype, though. So he turned again to a trusted friend for
advice: Andre told him to be patient. "You're going to get
your opportunities," he said. "When you get out there,
don't force yourself, just play your game. Larry's a basketball great. Give him the ball, play some defense, and don't

worry about your own output, worry about making the team better."

Reggie heeded the guidance. "I just try to stay focused on what's going on," he said. "Right now this team belongs to Larry and the others. They've won the championships. I know one day I will fill their roles. My time will come."

With Reggie about to enter the final year of his contract, the Celtics knew it was time to negotiate a new deal if they wanted to keep him. He was set to earn $400,000, paltry pay by NBA standards. But team executives concentrated instead on wrapping up an agreement with holdout Brian Shaw. They assumed that Reggie's situation could wait, and that it could be handled easily later. That was a mistake. "The Celtics weren't taking me seriously," Reggie said. "They needed to know I was serious." Reggie hired controversial agent Jerome Stanley, and, by doing so, put the Celtics on notice that he intended to get the most he could for his talent. "People have always seen me as a shy kid who doesn't say much," Reggie said. "I think people took me for granted."

That quietness led some to believe Reggie was a pushover. Coach Calhoun says though that Reggie had "an inner strength that most people never saw."

Stanley indicated that he might not even negotiate with the Celtics — that Reggie might play in Europe instead. The warning shots worked. The Celtics became intent on nailing down a new contract for their swingman. Late in the afternoon on August 21, 1990, Reggie called a news conference in the Celtics office. "I'm not happy at all," he said. He insisted he had enjoyed his years with the Celtics, but he

made one statement repeatedly: "What I'm going to do is ful-
fill the year on my contract. Then I'm going to do what's
best for me." At the very same time, however, Stanley and
the Celtics brass were behind closed doors putting the
finishing touches on a new contract.

Less than two hours after his news conference, Reggie
was back in front of the microphones. This time he was all
smiles. He had just signed an astonishing five-year contract
extension worth more than three million dollars a year. The
deal made him one of the five highest-paid players in the
NBA. "I'm very happy to have all this behind me," he said.
"Now, I want to set my sights on helping the team bring
another NBA championship to Boston." Reggie said he
knew the negotiations were in progress when he spoke to
reporters earlier, but he "was surprised they reached an
agreement so fast. It just shows how big a part of the
Celtics' future I am."

Reggie also began playing a major role in the Boston
community, even as he maintained a connection to his
hometown of Baltimore. He wasn't satisfied with quick
appearances at photo opportunities. He became genuinely
involved in a number of programs for young people. Some
of his favorites were the summer basketball camps and
leagues he helped sponsor.

At the start of the Reggie Lewis-Harbor Point basketball
camp at the University of Massachusetts-Boston, Reggie
spoke to the TV crews for a few minutes. Then he shooed
them away. "That's it," he said. "I have to go spend time
with the kids." And he spent hours each day of the camp,
teaching skills and talking to the kids about basketball and

life. Rodney Hughes, a coach at the University who helped operate the camp, mentioned to Reggie that there would be no trophies at the end of the week. There was only enough money to buy a few, he said, and none of the children should be left out. Reggie told Rodney he would pay for trophies for all 250 kids who attended. It was a pledge he kept each year.

Reggie once promised the kids at the camp he would give them NBA posters, but when he arrived the next day, he had forgotten to bring the box with him. Rather than disappoint any of the children, he drove back home, returned with the posters, and took the time to autograph one for each camper. Reggie also sent posters plus sneakers and other equipment to the Cecil-Kirk recreation center in Baltimore to be distributed to the children there.

The Reggie Lewis Summer League was a basketball program for young people based at the Shelburne Community Center in Roxbury. The head of the center, Alfreda Harris, says Reggie was a great role model for young black men. "He was as gentle and kind a person as you would meet," she said. "He was a total man."

Reggie also took part in the National Youth Sports Camps that Rodney directed at UMass/Boston. "He would participate in all the sports — except basketball," Rodney says. "I wanted it that way so everyone would see how great an athlete he was at other sports."

The charitable event most associated with Reggie was his Annual Turkey Giveaway. Needy people filled out entry forms, and several hundred were chosen. Reggie carefully reviewed all the forms and handed out each turkey personally.

The tradition began during the holiday season of 1990, when Reggie gave out 300 turkeys at Roxbury Community College in Boston. Then he went home to distribute turkeys at the Cecil-Kirk center. That day was officially declared Reggie Lewis Day in the City of Baltimore. Mayor Kurt Schmoke called Reggie a Baltimore hero "whose community service work had a more positive effect on inner-city teenagers than most government programs."

Reggie got a call from Baltimore one evening. It was his friend Joe Dickens.

"Why don't you come on up?" Reggie said.

"I won't have enough money until tomorrow," Joe replied.

"Don't worry. Go to the airport, and I'll have a ticket waiting for you."

Joe flew to Boston and spent a wonderful weekend hanging out with Reggie. One evening they went to a local shopping mall. They were both wearing white sweat suits. It didn't take long for Reggie to be noticed.

"Wow! That's Reggie Lewis! Can I have your autograph?"

Reggie kept walking as he was signing. Some of the fans who followed along asked: "Who's that with you? Does he play pro ball?"

"Yeah," said Reggie.

"Who does he play for?"

"A team on the west coast."

"All right!" they said, and they began asking Joe for *his* autograph, too. Reggie had given the man who helped introduce him to basketball a taste of what it was like to be an NBA star. Joe was ecstatic. "I felt so good!" he said.

The Celtics had no cause to regret spending megabucks to re-sign Reggie. He proved his worth. During the 1990-91 season, he boosted his scoring output and also his popularity among the fans. In the Celtics' eleven-game play-off run, he averaged over 22 points per game. Reggie did all this despite a lower back injury that bothered him for a good part of the season. He could often be seen on the bench applying heat to the sore area.

The days of cramped studio apartments were over for Donna and Reggie. They moved into a spacious, modern home surrounded by trees in the Boston suburb of Dedham. Mark lived right down the street, so he saw Reggie frequently. With Andre now playing professional basketball in Australia most of the year, Mark had become Reggie's best friend.

They found each other's company to be a sure cure for anything that might be getting them down. "Reggie would sometimes stop by, and I would sense something was up," Mark says, "but we usually never got into it because by the end of the evening, we never really cared. If something was bothering either of us, we both agreed not to bug the other person about it." Mark says he and Reggie rarely saw the need to have a serious talk. "He liked to have a good time, he liked to be around people, and he liked to laugh."

Reggie was far from idle in the off-season. He did strength training exercises and stretching exercises, with special attention to his back. In long solo workouts, he practiced his dribbling. And with help from a former Northeastern player, he worked on becoming better at stealing the ball.

One hot day in July, the phone rang in Mark's house. It was Reggie calling. "Hey, I'm going to Vegas," he said, matter-of-factly. "What are you doing next week?"

That was Reggie's way of telling his friend that he and Donna were going to get married. Reggie never actually asked Mark to be his best man, but Mark could read between the lines. "It was out of the blue," Mark says. "But it wasn't a complete surprise."

Reggie and Donna had been living together for years, so they decided they did not want a big, formal wedding ceremony. They preferred something casual and quick, with just their closest friends.

Reggie called Peggy to break the news to her. "Mama, we're going to Las Vegas to get married."

"You're what? Why would you want to go and do something like that?"

"Donna and I decided to do it this way instead."

"What happened to your plans of coming to Baltimore for your wedding? I'd like to be there when you're married."

"I'm sorry; this is just the way we want it."

Donna, Reggie, and Mark flew to Las Vegas. They were joined there by Donna's best friend and another acquaintance, a friend of Brian Shaw's who happened to be in town. The wedding was to be just a brief interlude in what was really a long weekend vacation. "It was probably the best time I've ever had in my life," Mark says. "Everything went right."

They stayed at the Flamingo Hotel. For a couple of days, Mark and Reggie hung out together, as did Donna and her friends. The ceremony was held at one of the many little wedding chapels scattered among the casinos and high-rise hotels in Las Vegas. At the moment the marriage became final, Reggie glanced at Mark. "He gave me a smile and a little bit of a look," Mark says, "a look that said, 'I did it' or 'did I do the right thing?' I kind of shrugged my shoulders in response." The whole group then went to dinner at Caesar's Palace. "Reggie was happy most of the time," Mark says, "but he really seemed to be in a good place during that trip."

Together, Reggie and Donna placed a call to Peggy.

"It's official! We're married, Ma," Reggie said.

After a long silence Peggy said, "If you're happy, I'm happy."

But Peggy was definitely not happy. "I was so disappointed not being able to be there," she says. The wedding was one of a series of events that caused a widening rift between Peggy and her son and new daughter-in-law.

Peggy's health was in jeopardy. She had suffered another heart attack the previous year, and she remained dependent on cocaine. Reggie didn't want to believe it, but Donna pointed out all the evidence of his mother's addiction to him: Peggy's dramatic mood changes, her weight loss, her inability to pay her bills although she was earning a decent salary.

Peggy realized she was on a dead-end path. She decided she wanted to quit taking drugs, and she called Reggie for help.

"Son, I want you to know that I have a drug problem."

"I know. Donna told me. I was just waiting for you to say something about it."

Reggie and Donna arranged for Peggy to enter a drug rehabilitation center in New York at their expense. The plan was for her to complete the program there, then go to work for a new charitable foundation that was being set up in Reggie's name. A staff member at the center told Peggy she would be admitted as soon as they received her medical records. Based on that statement, Peggy quit her job to prepare to enter treatment. After reviewing her records, however, the center did an about-face. Peggy's application was rejected. She was told the program was "too stressful" for her, given her heart condition.

Peggy was floored. When she called Reggie's house, she expected some compassion. What she got instead was a confrontation. Donna was agitated. "She said, 'Why did you quit your job before you heard definitely from the center?'" Peggy recalls. "I explained that they had assured me I could start the program when they got my records." Tempers flared, and by the end of the conversation, both women were upset.

Reggie tried to calm the emotions. He told Peggy, "Ma, find yourself another program, and I'll pay for it. I'll take care of you." Peggy was too furious to listen. She felt that her daughter-in-law had treated her disrespectfully, and as a result she was angry not just with Donna but with Reggie, as well.

"I don't want you taking care of anything!" Peggy snapped at Reggie. "I'll handle it myself."

Peggy reacted to the blowup by going on a month-long intoxication binge. Finally, she mustered the courage to take control of her life.

With help from Reggie's friend Joe, Peggy found a drug rehabilitation center operated by the Salvation Army in Wilmington, Delaware. She entered the program in January 1992 and paid for her room and board by working in a nearby factory warehouse. Peggy also began taking academic courses in what little free time she had because she wanted to earn a high school equivalency degree. One day, she thought, Reggie would be as proud of her as she was of him.

In the first season under his new multimillion dollar contract, Reggie was noticeably more relaxed and confident in his playing. "I really feel I can take anybody one-on-one," he said. "That's my strength. I can beat people off the dribble." Reggie focused on improving other areas of his game. "I'm trying to be more aggressive on the defensive end. I'm starting to roam around a bit to help guys out." Another priority was keeping his back healthy. Robert Parish taught him some martial arts-type stretches that helped a great deal.

Reggie was recognized as one of the top two dozen players in the world when he was named to the NBA All-Star team. He was thrilled by the honor. "I've now reached one of my goals," he said. "I've still got a big one left: to win an NBA championship." Reggie remembered watching the All-Star games on TV each year as a youngster. "I saw all the premier players who were selected," he said. "I thought it was something special." Reggie's All-Star status made it absolutely clear that the "sixth man" was now first among his former Dunbar teammates, none of whom had achieved such prominence as a pro. "They all had bigger reputations than me in high school, and they played for high profile college programs," Reggie said. "But that only made me work that much harder to make a name for myself."

As the season progressed, Reggie kept getting better. Celtics coach Chris Ford said, "Reggie has become an NBA player beyond our wildest dreams. At guard or forward, wherever he plays, I know he's going to do a lot of damage."

Many opposing players seconded that opinion. "He's beyond All-Star," said Orlando Magic center Stanley Roberts. "He's All-Pro. He's got 'greatest' written all over him."

Reggie became the first Celtic since Dave Cowens in the '70's to lead the team in steals, blocks, and scoring in the same season. In characteristic style, he intensified his performance during the play-offs, averaging 28 points in ten contests. He scored 36 twice, in the Eastern Conference quarterfinals and semifinals, and he poured in 42 points in the Celtics' close semifinal loss to Cleveland.

After a play-off game against Indiana, Mark met Reggie in the tunnel of the Boston Garden. Reggie had done well, and he was smiling. Up came Reggie Miller of the Pacers. "You better tell your coach to double team me," he said with a swagger. "You had a tough time stopping me."

Reggie stayed cool. "You did get yours tonight. But I'll tell you what. You're having a difficult time stopping me, too."

What amazed Mark was that even when Reggie did not have a good game, he still came out of the locker room in a great mood. "I would ask him why he had a smile on his face after he had shot poorly, and he'd say, 'We have another game tomorrow, and I bet I'll make more than thirty points.'"

Karl Fogel says Reggie had the most resilient personality of any player he has ever coached. "He could have three shots blocked and miss ten in a row," Fogel says, "and believe he would make the next ten." Reggie was convinced that if he had a bad day, he would always bounce back.

Reggie may have gotten that resilience from his mother. Peggy completed the intensive program at the rehabilitation center in three months. She broke her addiction and has stayed off drugs completely ever since. She also emerged with a deep sense of connection to God.

Peggy phoned Reggie to tell him what she had accomplished. Although Donna was said to be skeptical that Peggy could have weaned herself from cocaine so quickly, Reggie was happy for his mother. He had prayed for years that she would give up drugs. Now that she had, he told her how proud he was of her.

The respect Reggie had sought for so long as a player was finally his. He had laid to rest all the doubts and judgments. "Reggie became the consummate professional — a pro's pro," Andre says. "He never forgot where he came from." The NBA didn't change him, and he wasn't distracted by the glitter. He concentrated on constantly improving himself and his game. A national TV advertisement for Reebok starring Reggie served to underscore the fact that he was now one of the elite players in the NBA.

The scene is a basketball court. Reggie is making a slew of slam dunks: forward jam, backward jam, and his dramatic reverse jam, only this time, through the magic of television,

Reggie is seen soaring upside down above the rim as he rams the ball through the net. While walking off the court, he looks at the camera and says, "That's Reggie." He pauses. Then, so there's no mistake, he adds, "Lewis."

One of the other Reggie's, Reggie Williams, says he really didn't get to know his Dunbar teammate while they were in high school. As pros, though, he says they became friends and frequently went out to dinner after their teams played each other. "We didn't really discuss basketball much. We talked instead about our years at Dunbar and about our old neighborhoods."

Back in East Baltimore, the Collington Square basketball court was badly in need of repair, so Reggie enlisted the help of Reebok in refurbishing it. The makeover included new backboards and nets and a freshly painted and lined court surface. Reggie flew in to take part in the dedication ceremony. A throng of young people watched Reggie put his footprints in a square of cement at the gate and cut the ribbon to reopen the court.

As part of the festivities, Coach Wade spoke to the crowd. He had made a mistake, he told them. Then he turned to Reggie and said, "I guess I should have started you."

"You're right," Reggie said without cracking a smile. "You should have."

Chapter Six
Final Challenge

Reggie had come a long way from East Baltimore. He was recognized. He was a role model. While he didn't revel in all the attention, he did enjoy it. At the Boston Garden and at public appearances, his fans greeted him with a chant: "Reggie, Reggie, Reggie."

He was hearing that same chant now, only in different accents. Reggie, accompanied by several other NBA stars, was on a summer tour of Europe for a corporate sponsor. In Portugal, Finland, and Greece, he had conducted basketball clinics and signed hundreds of autographs. Next stop: Paris, France.

The setting was perfect. A vast parking area covered with a forest of basketball goals brought in for the occasion. In the background was a photogenic French chateau. The only problem was the weather. It was pouring rain.

The crowd was soaked but excited. They struck up the chant as Reggie arrived and was hustled into a nearby holding tent. He was advised to wait there for a break in the weather and the arrival of some other players, who had been delayed by the storm. But the people outside kept chanting, and Reggie got restless.

He stepped out onto the stage set up for the event, and he was instantly drenched. When the fans (mainly kids) caught sight of him, they cheered even louder. Reggie took his time greeting them with handshakes and high fives.

"I really felt bad for all the kids out there," Reggie said. "It really was amazing to hear them chanting my name like that. I just felt like I had to go out there and do it. They got a big kick out of it. So did I. It was the right thing to do."

Doing the right thing was Reggie's way. Financially, he was set for life, but he still wanted to complete his academic work at Northeastern and earn his degree in criminal justice. He took two of the required courses during the summer and planned to finish the rest during subsequent off-seasons.

Reggie also expanded his already substantial community involvement. He became a spokesman for the Boys and Girls Clubs of Boston as well as for a group devoted to African-American young people. "I feel there's a need to help the kids," he said, "because a lot of them have chosen the wrong path. If I can change that, it would be great."

NBA coach and former player John Lucas organized a celebrity tennis tournament in Houston to benefit his anti-drug work. Reggie accepted an invitation to participate although he had never really played the game. Just going through the motions was not his style; he wanted to make a good showing. Reggie arranged to have several lessons at Northeastern. To insure he would have a playing partner, he entered Mark in the tournament, and the two of them practiced frequently. "We became halfway decent," Mark says.

They would sometimes play all day at the local public tennis courts.

The better they became, the more heated their games got. "It reached the point where we would really go at it," Mark says. Just as with basketball, though, Reggie kept the competition in proper perspective. His favorite saying was: "Don't take it personally. You'll still be my friend — after I beat you."

Reggie had to cancel out of the tournament (although he continued playing tennis) because of a momentous event in his life: the birth of his first child. Donna and Reggie named their son Reggie, Jr. They were proud parents, and Reggie basked in the delights of fatherhood. "The happiest I ever saw him was when little Reggie was born," says Celtics vice-president M.L. Carr. "He was so good with everybody else's kids. That's why God blessed him with a son."

There was another important occurrence that August, one affecting Reggie's professional life. Larry Bird retired from the Boston Celtics due to chronic back problems. Coach Ford went to the team's two elder statesmen, Robert Parish and Kevin McHale, to sound them out about the role of captain. Both told him that Reggie was the man to lead the team into the future, and Ford agreed.

"Reggie is a great guy and a great player," McHale said. "A huge part of the responsibility of the team will fall directly on his shoulders."

Reggie was ready for the challenge. "I'm really looking forward to it," he said. "I'll have to be more of a leader on the floor and help out defensively. I am being more vocal than I have in the past. I know I have a lot to prove."

Reggie admitted he wouldn't be as outspoken as Bird, but he promised to bring his own style of leadership to the job. "I do my talking by going to practice early, by diving for loose balls," he said. "And when guys see you playing hurt, they respect you."

Getting used to the new title took a little while. Parish called for the captain once during practice. Reggie automatically looked around for Bird, then he realized The Chief was talking to him.

McHale predicted that Reggie would have a "knockdown, drag-out, tremendous" year, but the regular season turned out to have more than its share of frustrations. There was some internal bickering among the players, and the team did not always function smoothly in games. Reggie felt responsible. "At first I think he liked being captain," Andre says, "but he wasn't always comfortable in the role. It didn't fit his personality."

For the second straight year, Reggie managed to lead the team in scoring with over 20 points per game. He failed to make the All-Star team, though, and he struggled with minor leg and back injuries. Several times during the season he reportedly suffered dizzy spells — always during home games and always right after he had come off a fast break. Each time, the wooziness passed quickly, and Reggie saw no cause for concern.

Increasingly, Donna took responsibility for handling Reggie's personal affairs, freeing him to devote his full attention to his game. She screened calls and interview requests and managed his appointment schedule and his finances. She was also involved with getting the Reggie

Lewis Foundation up and running. In addition, there were daily duties involved with raising their son. Reggie once told a friend, "I'd be lost without her." Donna was fiercely loyal to her husband and protective of his interests. But Reggie's mother and family in Baltimore felt they were losing touch with him.

The Celtics made it to the play-offs. Their first opponents would be the Charlotte Hornets. Reggie was looking forward to the games to make up for a regular season that he called the worst of his career. He wanted to prove he could lead the team to an NBA championship, like Larry Bird and the other legendary Celtics captains before him. He also had another incentive to be at his best. This would be the first play-off showdown between Reggie and two of his former Dunbar teammates: Muggsy Bogues and David Wingate.

Though the days when they competed in the Baltimore recreation league seemed light years away, each still knew what the others could do. "I know all of Truck's moves, every one," Muggsy said. "I know where he likes to score, where he likes to receive the ball. And I know if we want to stop him, we have to make him work constantly and tire him out."

Reggie was just as familiar with Muggsy's distinctive playing style. "He's doing the same things he's always done," Reggie said. "He pushes the ball as fast as he can. He goes to the hole, looks like he's driving, but I know he's going to pass. I always play him to pass."

'Gate acknowledged that the way he used to play Reggie defensively might not work anymore. "I saw him every day, every summer, for a long, long time," he said. "But Reggie has improved a lot. Sometimes he's almost unstoppable."

Before the start of post-season play, the team physician, Dr. Arnold Scheller, ran treadmill tests on the Celtics. Reggie passed with no problem. Routine electrocardiograms done by the team each year since 1990 showed Reggie to have an abnormal heartbeat, but follow-up tests always came out normal.

On Thursday, April 29, 1993, the Celtics were preparing for the first game of the series at the Boston Garden. Reggie was usually cool, calm, and collected both before and during games. Other than an occasional smile after a dramatic dunk, he rarely showed much emotion. This night was different, though. His teammates had never seen him so fired up. "I just figured he was pumped because, for the first time, it was going to be his play-off, not Larry's," said Kevin McHale. Reggie paced and fidgeted. Some of his buddies even teased him because they thought he was nervous. That wasn't it at all. He was just eager for the contest to begin. There was a look of intensity in his eyes.

During warm-ups, the three Dunbar alumni exchanged nods and smiles of greeting. Muggsy recalls a sense of exhilaration. "To see three people from the neighborhood we grew up in, just to make it in the NBA," he said, "then to make it to the play-offs together — to do something we had dreamed about as kids — was a great feeling."

From the opening tap, Reggie unleashed an awesome offensive barrage. He stung the Hornets with ten points in the first three minutes alone. "He was all over the place," Coach Ford said, "like a jet — scoring and running." The Chief grabbed a rebound and the Celtics headed downcourt, with Reggie angling toward the lane on the left side.

Suddenly, the jet did a nosedive.

As he approached the three-point line, Reggie felt faint. He stumbled and fell forward to one knee, then his momentum carried him down face-first onto the parquet floor. His right fist made a thud as it hit the polished wood. Reggie turned over and sat up, looking dazed.

He reached for his chest.

For several seconds, play continued around Reggie. Donna leaped out of her seat and shouted at Coach Ford to alert him.

"Chris! Something's wrong with Reggie!"

Once time was called, Reggie stood up. His head was now clear, but his legs felt rubbery. Slowly, he walked toward the bench.

Dr. Scheller wasn't worried. He thought Reggie had been elbowed in the head. Reggie rested for three minutes and returned to the game. After just one minute of playing, however, he felt lightheaded again. He was taken out and sent to the trainer's room, where Donna visited him.

During the halftime break, Dr. Scheller and Celtics chief executive officer Dave Gavitt reviewed a videotape and saw clearly that Reggie had collapsed without being hit. Scheller checked Reggie's vital signs and found them to be normal.

Reggie went out onto the court to participate in a Boys Club presentation. He then ran up and down the floor a few times to test his legs. When he came back to the locker room, he told Scheller he felt better and wanted to play. The doctor agreed to allow him to start the second half.

Gavitt was skeptical. "Are you 100 percent sure?" he asked Scheller. "If you're not, I'll make the call right now that he doesn't play." Scheller assured Gavitt that he was comfortable with the decision, and he promised to keep a close eye on Reggie.

The crowd was cheering loudly as Reggie headed for the Celtics bench at the end of halftime. But the ovation was not for him. There was no acknowledgment of his courage for returning. The fans were chanting "Larry! Larry!" for Larry Bird, who was just taking his seat in the stands.

As if to show his predecessor who was now in charge, Reggie picked up his scoring binge where he had left off in the first quarter. He opened with two big fallaway jumpers. He added a foul shot. About six minutes into the half, he had just released a shot when he again felt a strange discomfort in his chest. He played on, following his miss with a rebound and conversion.

Over on the bench, some of Reggie's teammates began to notice that his legs looked wobbly. They alerted Coach Ford, who immediately called for a timeout. Reggie made a slight motion with his hand. It was a sign that he wanted out. No one could remember Reggie ever asking to leave a game before, but he was dizzy again, and he knew he needed to sit down.

He was assisted to the bench. An ice pack was placed on the back of his neck, and he was handed a towel, which he held to his mouth. The team trainer told him to take slow, deep breaths. He never went back in.

In 13 total minutes of playing time, Reggie had scored 17 points. It was one of the most spectacular performances of his basketball career. He had no way of knowing at the time it was also the final performance.

After the game, while the Celtics celebrated their victory, Dr. Scheller checked Reggie's vital signs again. They were normal. Although Scheller was concerned, he felt Reggie was in no immediate danger. He told him to get some rest and to come to New England Baptist Hospital the next day for tests.

Reggie left the Garden in a hurry with Donna at his side. Both looked visibly shaken. Reggie admitted his collapse during the game had scared him. "I started having flash-backs to that Hank Gathers thing," he said. Gathers was the Loyola Marymount star who died shortly after collapsing on a basketball court in 1990 as a result of a heart ailment.

The Celtics asked for a quick readout on Reggie's condition so they would know whether he could play in Saturday's game. Four of the first six tests conducted on Reggie at the hospital suggested that he had a potentially deadly defect at the bottom of his heart. One of the proce-dures, a type of stress test, revealed what appeared to be some areas of dead heart tissue.

Reggie went home in the afternoon, but a message on his beeper summoned him back to the hospital later that day. Doctors wanted to run another test — a risky one — in which a catheter is inserted directly into the heart. The results showed that part of Reggie's lower left heart chamber was not moving in sync with the rest. An additional test was scheduled at another hospital the next day, but the decision was made to keep Reggie at New England Baptist overnight so his heart could be monitored.

Just before dawn Saturday, the regular blips on the instruments attached to Reggie's chest changed briefly into a jagged pattern. An alarm tone was triggered. The monitor had registered a series of six irregular heartbeats within the space of a few seconds.

As a precaution, a portable monitor was used to keep tabs on Reggie as he was transferred to the Deaconess Hospital for his magnetic resonance imaging test. The cardiac MRI produced dramatic video images that showed a defect in the same area of the lower left heart wall pointed out in other tests.

Dr. Scheller knew the results were foreboding. To get the most accurate diagnosis possible, he decided to assemble a group of top cardiac specialists, a panel he dubbed "the dream team." Scheller was unaware of the irony. He had no idea what that name meant to Reggie.

The panel of doctors gathered Sunday afternoon at New England Baptist while Reggie and Donna waited upstairs in his hospital room. For two hours the physicians reviewed Reggie's medical records and test results. Drug use was brought up as one of the possible causes of the type of heart damage the tests revealed. Although some remained skeptical, Dr. Scheller assured the specialists that Reggie had absolutely no history of drug use.

It took the dream team surprisingly little time to arrive at a unanimous working diagnosis: focal cardiomyopathy, damage to the heart muscle wall at the bottom of Reggie's heart. The condition was potentially life-threatening. Reggie's pro basketball career appeared to be at an end.

Dave Gavitt and another Celtics executive, Jan Volk, were listening at the back of the room. They were shocked by what they heard. When the meeting broke up, they rushed from the hospital to catch the team's charter flight to Charlotte without stopping to say a word to Reggie.

That left Dr. Scheller to deliver the news. When he arrived at Reggie's room, Mark and Donna were there. Mark stepped outside. Scheller carefully explained the diagnosis and the seriousness of the condition. Reggie appeared calm, but both he and Donna felt overwhelmed. They asked to speak to a cardiologist. On his way out, Scheller handed them a copy of a press release he said was being sent to the news media.

The reaction in the room was a mixture of strong emotions. Reggie and Donna were deeply disturbed by the diagnosis. They were disillusioned with the dream team because they felt excluded from the deliberations. They were angry with the Celtics, especially after the hasty departure by Gavitt and Volk. And they were upset with the doubting doctors who kept asking Reggie whether he had used cocaine in spite of his insistence that he had not. Donna says the doctors never requested that Reggie take a drug test. If he had been asked, she says, he would have complied.

Donna called a friend, George Kaye, who was an administrator at nearby Brigham and Women's Hospital and complained about the way Reggie was being treated. He put her in contact with Dr. Gilbert Mudge, the director of clinical cardiology at Brigham and Women's, who agreed to take Reggie's case. A late-night transfer was arranged, but no one bothered to warn the staff at New England Baptist.

At around 11 p.m., Donna returned to Reggie's room with her administrator friend in tow. They joined Mark in helping Reggie get packed. Reggie signed a waiver form, then he peeled off the three adhesive patches that held heart monitor leads to his chest. His nurses were dumbfounded.

After putting on sweat pants and a Celtics jersey turned inside out, Reggie headed for the door. He and Mark tried to sneak out a side entrance, but a reporter saw them and asked what was going on. "I'm just out to get some fresh air," Reggie joked. He climbed into a waiting Brigham and Women's security van for the short trip to the other hospital.

The next day, reporters tracked down Dr. Scheller in Charlotte, and he gave them his blunt reaction to the transfer. He said that Reggie and Donna were "in denial" about the heart condition, and that in the opinion of the specialists Reggie's playing days were probably over. Scheller's remarks just aggravated Reggie's sense of alienation from the Celtics.

One of Reggie's first visitors as he rested at Brigham and Women's was Coach Calhoun. They chatted about the Hornets game. "You would have gotten 50 shots that night," Calhoun said.

Reggie laughed. "Coach, I was going to make every shot." Calhoun stayed for several hours. The mood was somewhat somber. The Coach sensed that Reggie was coming to grips with the idea that he might never be able to play basketball again.

At Brigham and Women's, Reggie got the kind of personal attention he felt he had been denied at New England Baptist. Dr. Mudge talked to Reggie several times a day and had already begun putting him through a new battery of tests.

Reggie told Mudge that he wanted to keep playing, and Mudge dedicated himself to finding a way to make that possible. In fact, the early test results suggested to Mudge that Reggie's medical condition might not be as serious as first thought. When Reggie heard this, he immediately became much more upbeat.

Among the phone calls from well-wishers was one from Australia. It was Andre. Reggie smiled when he heard the voice at the other end of the line. The connection was poor, so Reggie spoke up.

"'Dre, are you still busting up those kangaroos down there?"

"Oh yeah! How are you doing? What's up?"

"There's nothing wrong with me. I'm all right."

"Are you going to be able to play?"

"Yeah, man. Don't believe any of those reports."

That was just like Reggie, Andre thought. Putting everybody at ease despite what he may have been feeling himself. Reggie told Andre he'd like to come to Australia later in the summer with Donna and Reggie, Jr., to get away from the news media spotlight.

Dr. Mudge assembled his own group of experts to consider Reggie's case. He was convinced that the dream team, under pressure to come up with a quick diagnosis, had reached the wrong conclusions about Reggie's condition.

In speaking to Mudge, Reggie mentioned that his brother Jon had undergone open-heart surgery as a child, but he did not go into detail about the family's extensive history of heart trouble. He did briefly discuss the series of dizzy spells he had suffered during the past season.

Not quite a week after Reggie had arrived at Brigham and Women's, Dr. Mudge scheduled a news conference to announce his dramatically-different diagnosis. Reggie had only a benign fainting condition, he said, not a life-threatening heart problem. The condition could be controlled with medication. "I am confident," Mudge said, "he can return to professional basketball without limitations." Reggie and Donna looked relieved and happy. So did Celtics executive Gavitt, who was quick to embrace Mudge's findings. "It was such good news," said Coach Calhoun. "It was the kind of good news we all wanted to believe."

Reggie wasn't the only one in his family who was dealing with a medical problem. Peggy learned that she had a blockage in a major artery that needed attention, but she was in danger of losing her health insurance because she was behind on the payments.

Peggy, Jon, and several other relatives traveled to Boston to visit Reggie, who was in great spirits after hearing Dr. Mudge's favorable analysis of his ailment. Reggie had just about dropped out of touch with his Baltimore family in recent months. But Peggy thought this might be an opportune time to ask her son if he would make the payments necessary to keep her medical insurance from being canceled. The total due was less than six hundred dollars. Reggie didn't hesitate. He said he would take care of it.

The next day was Mother's Day. Reggie called Peggy and told her that after talking to his wife, he had changed his mind. He would not make the payments on her medical insurance. He said Donna felt it was insensitive of her to give him a bill while he was lying on his sick bed.

Peggy was speechless.

She had debated whether to ask the favor of him and did so only when she was assured his condition was not serious. As for Donna's role in his turnabout, Peggy told her son, "You do not need anyone to speak for you or make your decisions. You are the one."

At the end of the conversation, almost as an afterthought, Reggie said, "Oh, by the way, happy Mother's Day." Peggy felt deeply hurt. Her sister Cookie says that was the low point in Peggy's relationship with Reggie.

The strain of coping with Reggie's uncertain medical situation was affecting everyone involved. The euphoria that followed Dr. Mudge's announcement wore off, especially after some of his expert consultants began to distance themselves from the rosy diagnosis. Reggie and Donna wondered why Mudge's conclusions were so completely at odds with those put forward by the dream team. They decided to get a third opinion.

In a conversation with Jon, Reggie reflected on the possibility of life without basketball. "I'll stay home and maybe build a pool," he said. "I don't need to play. I'm financially set. I'll be able to spend time with little Reggie."

Toward the end of June, Reggie flew to Los Angeles to be examined by a team of four specialists. After more tests, these doctors all agreed with Dr. Mudge that Reggie had a fainting condition. Three of the four also believed, though, that Reggie had a potentially serious heart defect: one part of his left ventricle was not moving in harmony with the rest. The California team was emphatic that Reggie should be monitored carefully during any physical activity.

Nearly two dozen doctors had now evaluated Reggie since his collapse. Rather than clarifying the situation, their myriad viewpoints perplexed Reggie. He was caught in what his agent called a crossfire of medical opinions. Reggie attended the Celtics' rookie camp at Brandeis University in mid-July, but he didn't play; he just watched.

Reggie was not yet ready to call it quits. He decided to continue preparing for a comeback while he sorted through the mountains of medical advice. For several weeks he had been following a light exercise schedule under Mudge's supervision, including free throws, and arm and leg lifts. Mudge had given his approval after Reggie did a workout while wearing a portable heart monitor. So far there had been no problems.

After two months off the basketball court, Reggie was eager to ease himself back into the game. On several July afternoons, he packed his gym bag and went to Brandeis to groove his jump shot. He shot three-pointers for an hour one day with the son of former Celtics star John Havlicek.

The plan was for Reggie to make his public comeback during the first week in August, although no one told the Celtics. Dr. Mudge was to be present to monitor the workout, and he would have a heart monitor and defibrillator courtside as a precaution.

The path was mapped out, but Reggie still had reservations. Coach Fogel had a chance to talk to his former Northeastern standout on the phone. Reggie sounded tense to him. "I'm certain he was torn about playing," he said. "He told me he was 97 percent sure he'd come back. That led me to believe it was really 50-50. An athlete normally talks about 110 percent when he's sure."

Reggie's usual determination was tempered by doubt. "The big question was, 'Should I play or shouldn't I play?'" Mark says. "If he were all set and ready to go, we would have spoken about it. He would have said, 'Mark, I'm ready to go.' But he didn't."

The concern Reggie was feeling led him to reach out to a past source of love and support: his family in Baltimore. "He started calling again," says his sister, Sheron.

"That's where he was getting peace of mind," adds Jon. "He realized he had been drifting too far away from us." Reggie especially wanted to heal his relationship with his mother. "They began talking again and were starting to understand each other," Jon says. "It was definitely going in a positive direction."

Peggy and Reggie took a major step during a two-hour phone conversation on July 23. "It was the first really good talk we'd had in a long while," Peggy said. They were candid with each other, and they covered a wide range of subjects. Reggie asked Peggy about her recovery and whether she was still drug-free. Peggy told Reggie she felt he had become too insulated from his family.

"I'm your mother," she said. "There's nothing in this world you can't say to me yourself, even if I did something that you aren't happy with."

Peggy was speaking from her heart, and the words sunk in. Reggie said he planned to come to Johns Hopkins Hospital in a couple of weeks for further tests. While he was in Baltimore, he said, he was going to pay off the mortgages on Peggy's house and Sheron's.

"I'm going to be taking control of things again," he told Peggy, "and I'll be doing my own talking from now on. No one will be speaking for me or coming between me and you."

Peggy was pleased by what she heard. It was her last conversation with her son.

******

Despite his ambivalence about a comeback, Reggie was ready to add some intensity to his workouts. He invited several of the regulars at the Brandeis gym to join him there at 5:30 p.m. on July 27. As he left the house that day, Reggie said, "Donna, I'm going to shoot some ball."

Reggie arrived at the gym at about 4:15, along with a relative, Robert Harris. In the trainer's room, Reggie changed into shorts, a gray tee shirt, and sneakers. He was unable to locate a key to the Celtics locker room.

Harris stood under the basket to retrieve the ball as Reggie began his warmup by shooting jumpers. When young players came up to him, he'd give them high-fives and joke with them. Reggie seemed more relaxed and happy than he had been in days. He was sinking three-pointers and not even working up a sweat.

Shortly after five p.m., everything changed.

Reggie dropped to the floor, then he slumped over on his side. Brandeis student Amir Weiss was shooting baskets on the next court over. "I heard this large sound," he said, "the sound of someone gasping for air. I looked over and saw Reggie on the floor, trying to breathe."

The noise was so striking that the others in the gym stopped what they were doing and gathered around to see what was happening. Among them was Rhonda Schafer, an Emergency Medical Technician, who was there with a group of kids from the summer camp where she worked.

Reggie's arms were limp. He looked half-conscious. Harris was holding him up in a sitting position. When Schafer asked Harris if he needed some help, he waved her off, insisting that Reggie was just tired.

She walked away, not wanting to intrude. In a few moments, though, she returned. "Look, I'm an EMT," she said. "Are you sure?" Harris now hesitated. He said he didn't know if Reggie was breathing. Schafer checked quickly and found that Reggie had a strong pulse but that his breathing was irregular.

"We have to lay him down," she said.

Schafer worked on reviving Reggie while two of her campers went for help. There was no need for CPR at this point, she decided, because he was still breathing.

At 5:13 p.m., the first call went out for an ambulance. Reggie's breathing was becoming more labored, and his pulse was almost imperceptible. His eyes were open, but he was clearly unconscious. Two Brandeis police officers who had arrived began performing CPR under Schafer's supervision, but she was not optimistic. "I don't think any person would have had the ability to save his life," she says. "I don't think it was in the cards."

By 5:20 p.m., two ambulance crews were on the scene, working feverishly on Reggie. They inserted a breathing tube and used a portable defibrillator to try to jolt his heart back into a normal beat. But Reggie was not responding. The decision was made to rush him to nearby Waltham-Weston Hospital. The paramedics radioed ahead, and Dr. Mary Anne McGinn, the only physician on duty in the emergency room, braced the staff.

By the time Reggie was wheeled into the hospital, the phones were already ringing, and people were milling about in the hallways. "There was pandemonium," said McGinn. The emergency room team went into action. McGinn ordered a wide range of tests to see if Reggie might be suffering from something other than heart failure. "We were hoping the problem was something we could fix," she said. If it was his heart, she realized, there was little chance at this point that Reggie could be revived. The paramedics who worked on him at the gym had the best chance, and they failed to get a reaction.

In Dedham, Donna had just returned to the house when the phone rang. It was Jimmy Myers, a family friend who was a local radio talk show host. The answering machine snared the call, but when Donna heard Myers' voice, she picked up the phone.

"Jimmy, I've got something to tell you. I'm going to be a mommy!" Donna had gotten word that she was pregnant. There was excitement in her voice. Rather than congratulations, though, she heard silence at the other end of the line. She knew something was wrong.

Myers asked her to brace herself. "We're living this nightmare again," he told her. "You have to get over to Waltham-Weston."

The heart monitor hooked to Reggie twice registered a rhythm briefly. All eyes in the room turned toward the blip bouncing across the screen. Each time, though, hope faded when no pulse was detected. In the absence of a pulse, the monitor reading meant the heart was merely generating electrical activity and not actually pumping. Dr. McGinn did not let up although she knew the odds were against her. She used every possible procedure that might do some good.

When Donna arrived, she was allowed into the treatment area to watch the emergency team work. She was also assigned a room nearby where she could have some privacy. In a separate room, members of the Celtics family were gathering, including Dave Cowens and M.L. Carr.

The intense effort to revive Reggie went on for nearly two hours. McGinn was willing to continue, but she knew there was now virtually no chance of success. She spelled out the situation to Donna, who listened closely.

"If what you're telling me is that it's hopeless," Donna said, "then let's stop." They did, at 7:30 p.m.

It took more than two hours to locate Peggy and notify her. Just after 10 p.m., Dr. McGinn walked into a hospital conference room crowded with reporters.

She announced the death of Reggie Lewis.

Chapter Seven

Remembering Reggie

It seemed like all of Boston turned out to say goodbye to Reggie. More than 15,000 people stood in line on St. Botolph Street, waiting to pay their final respects. Some were in dark suits or dresses; others wore shorts and sneakers. The crowd was a mosaic of races and ages. They moved four abreast into Matthews Arena and past Reggie's casket, which was surrounded by flowers. The site of some of Reggie's greatest basketball moments had been transformed into a place of tribute.

After the viewing, over 7,000 people jammed the arena for an emotional memorial service. They fanned themselves with their programs to cope with the sweltering heat. For the many who couldn't get in, the service was carried live on local TV stations. Northeastern University president John Curry set the tone for nearly two hours of eulogies when he said Reggie was "a young man who cared about other people. He was, quite simply, a beautiful person." Reggie's cousins Terry and Perry spoke, as did his brother Irvin, who said, "Reggie is in God's garden now."

The coach who first cultivated Reggie's basketball skills at Northeastern, Jim Calhoun, said, "Reggie was about simple things: wit, that special smile, the special comfort he

139

gave others. I may coach another great player; the Celtics will have another captain; but we'll never have another Reggie. We'll never forget him." Calhoun fought back tears as he looked down toward the open casket and said, "Thanks, Reggie. I love you."

Friend and former coach Keith Motley called on the crowd to "wake up the angels because they weren't expecting Reggie." He led them in a resounding chant of "Reggie, Reggie, Reggie."

The funeral procession followed a route designed by Donna to go through some of Boston's poorest neighborhoods. Thousands of people, many holding banners and signs with the number "35," lined the streets. In a private ceremony, Reggie was laid to rest at Forest Hills Cemetery.

Baltimore had its own farewell for Reggie several days later. There were fewer tears now; it was a time to celebrate not mourn. The Dunbar auditorium was crowded with aunts, uncles, cousins, and friends who had known Reggie since he was a child. Peggy sat in the front row, resplendent in a white suit.

Julia Woodland, the principal at Dunbar when Reggie was a student, smiled as she recalled his quiet nature. "I'd see him during the day and ask, 'Hey, Reggie, where are you going?' and this soft voice would come back, 'Oh, down the hall.'" Woodland said, "The roots of Reggie sprouted [in East Baltimore] and ultimately spread into a great forest. Reggie is the giant oak tree in that forest."

Printed in the program for the service was a poem to Reggie from his mother. It read in part:

The blow was hard; the shock severe.
I never thought of death so near.
But only those who have lost can tell
The pain of parting without a farewell.

On the way to Dunbar, the motorcade had stopped at Collington Square. The players on the court watched respectfully as Peggy placed a vase of pink roses at the patch of cement with Reggie's footprints and signature. Now the court was alive again with the sound of dribbling and balls swishing through nets as young people from a new generation worked on their games.

The next generation of Reggie's family got a new addition in February 1994. Donna gave birth to a girl whom she named Reggiena. With help from members of the Celtics, Donna has continued the Annual Reggie Lewis Turkey Giveaway. "Hopefully," she says, "I'll teach my children to carry on the tradition."

The Celtics agreed to pay the remainder of Reggie's contract to Donna, and his will listed her as his sole beneficiary. Reggie's estate has kept up mortgage payments on the houses where Peggy and Sheron live. Reggie wanted to bring about a healing of the divisions within his family. Without him present to be a catalyst, that process slowed, but it did not stop.

Reggie was just a few courses away from earning his degree from Northeastern when he died. In June 1994, the University held a ceremony to confer upon him posthumously the honorary degree of Doctor of Humanities. The diploma was accompanied by a citation:

"Intelligence, scoring talent, and the ability to motivate his teammates combined to create an athlete who could elevate a game to heights James Naismith himself could not have imagined possible. Although Reggie soared on the court, he remained grounded in life, always remembering those less fortunate. Just as his ear-to-ear grin lit up a room when he stepped in, his quiet generosity made the future brighter for so many."

The diploma was inscribed: "Reginald Lewis, Sr. — Gifted Athlete, Generous Philanthropist, Genuine Hero."

Reggie too had heroes: the people who offered him advice and guidance throughout his life. This network of friends, family members, and mentors was exceptional in its depth and loyalty.

"Everybody who was personally involved with him stayed with him," says Reggie's friend Joe Dickens. "Once we had grabbed him and took hold of him, we kept him, regardless of whom he went to next."

From Joe to Anthony Lewis at Cecil-Kirk, to Coach Calhoun, to friends like Andre LaFleur and Mark Reeves, Reggie always seemed to have someone near him who cared — someone who could serve as a sounding board and provide just the right balance of support, advice, and encouragement.

As a role model himself, Reggie reflected many of the values he had admired in others. Basketball for him was a way up, not a way out. He wanted to stay connected to the community. "Reggie never forgot where he came from," Anthony says. "He remembered the city, and he always took time to do little things. He gave back in so many ways."

Whenever Reggie offered to buy Joe a gift, Joe turned him down. "I'd tell him, 'If you want to give me something, give to my son what I've given to you: time and attention.' That's all I asked of him." And Joe says Reggie responded. "Not only did he give to my son, but also to hundreds of other kids, too."

Reggie's friend Mark works with inner city young people. When Reggie would come to visit, he'd speak to the kids from his own experience. Mark says, "He told them, 'It's normal to get frustrated. Don't quit. You're going to get a chance, and when you do, you've got to be ready.'" The advice applied to life, not just sports. He often told kids with dreams of NBA careers not to pin all their hopes on basketball.

That's the message Reggie gave Joe's son, Joe, Jr., who also happens to be Reggie's oldest nephew. "He would tell me, 'You aren't going to make it in life if you don't go to school, or study and read.'"

Reggie loved responding to challenges, and he encouraged others to do the same. "He was the kind of person that, if you were doing something with your life, he would help," Andre says. "But if you weren't, he wasn't going to support you. He wouldn't give something for nothing, no matter how much he loved the person."

Every time Reggie got together with his older brother, Irvin, he would say, "Show me something new." He wasn't talking about a new basketball move. Reggie wanted to know what Irvin was doing to better himself.

Reggie was constantly striving to improve his skills. Andre says, "Reggie was just the hardest working quiet achiever. He stayed focused on his goals, and he never complained." Those qualities endeared Reggie to many of his fellow NBA players.

"He wasn't worried about being a star," says Reggie Williams. "He just wanted to be part of the team and win. He understood what he wanted, and he went for it. He didn't tell the world he was great; he showed them."

The fact that Reggie was not flashy or controversial impressed Robert Parish. "He didn't have an overinflated opinion of himself, and that is rare in this business." Parish says Reggie's many excellent qualities should serve as a model for young people. "He had great character, and he did a lot for the less fortunate. But he never did anything for anyone because he had to. He just did it from the goodness of his heart."

Parish had a memorable experience of that kindness. "My youngest daughter once had a huge crush on Reggie," he says. "That's how much she cared about him. She hoped to have a chance to meet him. After one of our games, she was in a mass of people crowding around Reggie. He stopped and took time to talk to her and give her an autograph and a hug." Parish says his daughter was on cloud nine. "And at the time," he adds, "Reggie didn't even know she was my daughter. He helped every child feel special. He was a genuinely nice person."

That's the way Reggie's friends and family members remember him, too. "He was a kind and caring individual," Donna says, "and he was an intelligent and wise man."

"He never put himself on a higher level," says Mark. "We were always equals, even when we were talking about basketball. When he came over, you would never know he was a star." Mark can't recall ever arguing with Reggie. "All the time I spent with Reggie was happy time," he says. "Reggie was a perfect friend — who *just* happened to be a great basketball player."

Reggie was underestimated throughout his life because people didn't believe such a mild-mannered, humble person could be so awesome on the basketball court. He worked hard to earn the respect and recognition he deserved. Andre admits he would sometimes hold his breath when Reggie got the ball in a crucial game situation. "I'd think to myself, 'Oh, oh. He's going to be nervous.' Then he would go to the basket right in the heat of the game. He would put up something like a left-handed sweeping hook, and it would bounce off the glass and in. I mean, he would do these shots that would just amaze you."

Another friend and Northeastern teammate agrees. "Some of the things Reggie did, you couldn't practice," Wes Fuller says. "He was not a great post-up player, but when he wanted, he could post you up as if he were Kareem. Reggie didn't practice a hook, but when he had to make one, it went in."

Wes says Reggie was a shooting star who kept taking his
game to higher and higher levels. "I saw him nail half-court
shots like they were regular jumpers. Once, when we were
playing Ohio State, Reggie shot an air ball. He followed it
immediately with a dunk. He could hit a three-pointer as he
went out of bounds behind the backboard — up, over, and
in."

Reggie played so well at times, he shocked even himself.
"You could see it on his face," Wes says. "It was like he
was in some sort of zone. He couldn't explain what was
happening. Whatever he threw up went in." Wes says his
quiet friend was an ordinary person blessed with extraordinary talents and character. "Reggie was a gift from God that
was given to us for a short time to share."

Reggie knew how fortunate he was, and he was grateful.
"The smallest things were exciting to him," Wes says. "Just
to be alive; to perform. When you grow up in the inner city
like we did, you savor the successes."

Peggy still can't believe how much Reggie achieved. "I
pinch myself to this day," she says, "and I thank the Lord."
From the time Reggie was a teenager, Peggy taught him to
express his gratitude in prayer. "I would tell him, 'Never
forget to thank God for your blessings,'" she says. "'God
has looked down on all these people — all your buddies and
teammates — and He chose you. So make sure you get
down on your knees and thank Him.'"

"I will, Ma. I do," Reggie replied.

Peggy was amazed when the chaplain of the Celtics told
her that Reggie went to chapel before and after every game
to kneel and pray. Sometimes he was the only player there.

The people who knew Reggie are grateful, too — for his presence in their lives. Reggie's story is not a tragedy but a triumph: he lived his dream — and he showed others the way they can do the same. After he set goals, he reached them through a combination of determination, discipline, and focus. He let his actions do his speaking for him. Even the shortness of his life produced valuable lessons for his friends: Tommorrow is not promised to you. Make the most of every opportunity. Live and enjoy each day to the fullest.

Although his heart failed at an early age, Reggie had more than enough heart to touch the lives of thousands of people. He didn't just talk about the need for community service, he did something about it by constantly helping others. And he left a trail of happiness wherever he went.

The essence of Reggie Lewis was quiet grace. He was generosity and gentleness. He was confidence, calmness, and caring — wrapped up in a smile.

******

For he was part of all the best
That Nature loves and gives,
And ever more on Memory's breast
He lies and laughs and lives.

- Paul Laurence Dunbar (1872-1906)

Epilogue

Reggie's death triggered a flurry of finger-pointing, speculation, and second-guessing. The debate focused at first on the dueling medical diagnoses and Reggie's decision to continue planning a comeback. Over a year-and-a-half later, the controversy was rekindled by a *Wall Street Journal* story disputing the official autopsy conclusions and death certificate.

The autopsy found that Reggie's heart was "abnormal,... and extensively scarred." The immediate cause of death was listed as an irregular heartbeat associated with scarring and enlargement of the heart tissue, which resulted from an infection by adenovirus type 2. (This is a simple virus that is spread by coughing and sneezing.) The *Journal* article called the finding "medically nonsensical" and insinuated that Reggie's heart failure was linked to cocaine use.

Two of the doctors who were consultants on the autopsy were quoted by the *Journal* as saying the scarring was "consistent with" a cocaine-damaged heart, although there were no test results to back up such a judgment. The article did not mention the extensive history of heart trouble in Reggie's family.

Dr. Mudge told the *Journal* he had warned his star patient "that [cocaine] is the only thing that would explain what we're seeing," and he stressed that if Reggie was still using it, "he had to stop immediately." The article said the doctor and Reggie had this talk while sitting in Reggie's car in mid-July 1993. Earlier accounts of their conversation, however, made no reference to drugs.

The *Journal* article touched off a "feeding frenzy" among reporters eager to find a cocaine connection. Quoting a "medical source," the *Boston Herald* said Reggie confided to Mudge that he used cocaine "before every home game" to enhance his performance. Mudge's public diagnosis — that Reggie suffered only from a benign fainting condition — was a cover, the *Herald* story claimed, to give Reggie time to wean himself from drugs and to allow his heart to heal. No independent confirmation was ever offered for this theory. Experts say those closest to Reggie would certainly have noticed if he had used cocaine on a regular basis, as the story suggested, and there is no evidence that anyone ever did.

Derrick Lewis (no relation), a former college teammate who had known Reggie since childhood, told two newspapers that he had used cocaine with him several times. Lewis claimed Reggie was "an experimental user, like a lot of people." Within a few days, however, Lewis completely retracted his story. He then said that although he did party at times with Reggie, there were "no drugs, no cocaine."

The allegations made in *The Wall Street Journal* prompted the Commonwealth of Massachusetts to do a thorough investigation into Reggie's autopsy and cause of death. Chief medical examiner Dr. Richard Evans announced the results of the probe at a news conference. "Reggie Lewis' death was not caused by cocaine," he said, "nor was the damage to the heart at all typical of that known to be caused by cocaine usage. The toxicology [tests] performed at the time of death found no evidence of cocaine or other drug abuse." The investigation confirmed the autopsy's original conclusion that Reggie's heart had been weakened by a virus. Pathologists detected the genetic fingerprint of the virus in the tissue samples they analyzed. In addition, Evans said Reggie was born with two heart problems that could have contributed to his death. He suffered from a mild narrowing of the aorta, the main artery that carries blood from the heart, and a stretching and thinning of the mitral valve, which could allow blood to flow backward between the heart chambers. Evans blamed Reggie's death on "the totality" of these factors, which he said was "the best explanation that anyone will ever have as to why [Reggie] died."

As to whether Reggie ever used cocaine, perhaps his friend and Celtics teammate Dee Brown put it best. "The only person who knows is Reggie," he said, "and he's not here to defend himself."

But the people who knew Reggie well — his family members and closest friends — are unanimous. They all believe strongly that Reggie did not use drugs. Andre LaFleur, who was "as close as a brother" to Reggie, said, "I can say 100 percent: He never used them. I would bet my life on it."

Reggie was adamantly opposed to drugs throughout his life. "Because of my addiction," Peggy said, "he saw the effect of drugs — on me and on everyone in our family. He hated the whole idea of drugs. He didn't even like to take aspirin for headaches."

Donna echoed that opinion in a WBZ-TV interview. "Reggie had no interest in drugs whatsoever," she said. "That doesn't say he couldn't possibly have tried cocaine. But I doubt it very seriously." She told CBS, "Reggie led a clean and good life. He was a man of character."

The drug debate does not diminish Reggie's accomplishments or the love and admiration people felt for him. Northeastern University president John Curry said he has never known an athlete — professional or amateur — who did so much for the poor or the youth of a city. Robert Parish added, "Just look at the way Reggie carried himself through life — with a lot of pride and with genuine compassion for people." Reggie's greatest legacy may be the many young people whom he inspired. From Baltimore to Boston, they still scrawl his name or jersey number on their sneakers — and dream.

******

On March 22, 1995, the Celtics retired Reggie's number in an emotional halftime ceremony before a sellout crowd of fans. The scene on the court would have brought a smile to his face: Donna and Peggy stood side-by-side holding Reggie, Jr. and Reggiena. The two women took turns hoisting the banner with Reggie's number "35" to a place of honor high above the parquet floor of the Boston Garden.

Photo Album

Collington Square Park and the neighborhood where Reggie Lewis grew up in East Baltimore.

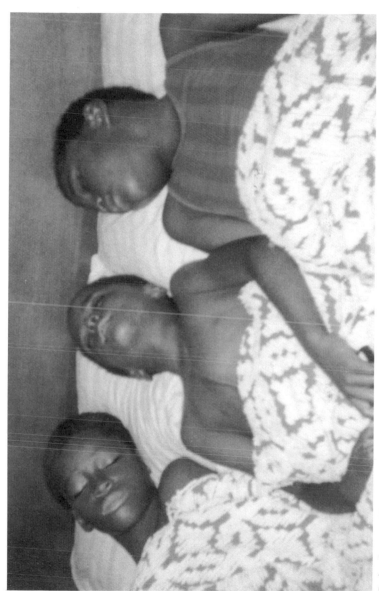

Irvin, Jon, and Reggie (age 6) take a break from jumping on the bed. (The scar on Jon's chest is from open-heart surgery.)

One of Reggie's many boyhood homes. The second floor was gutted by fire.

Reggie on the day he graduated from sixth grade.

The Cecil-Kirk Recreation Center.

Reggie at age 14, the year he started playing basketball in earnest at Cecil-Kirk.

Baltimore's Dunbar High School.

The 1982 Dunbar Poets. Front Row: Tim Dawson, Reggie Williams, Karl Wallace, Eric Green, Karl Amos, Darryl Wood, Muggsy Bogues. Back Row: Prieastly Reeves, Jerry White, Ellis Dorsey, Reggie Lewis, David Wingate, Gary Graham, Keith James, Keith Wallace.

Irvin, 17, and Reggie, 16, in front of their home.

Taresa Stewart and Reggie at the Dunbar High School senior prom in 1983.

Mark Reeves and Reggie after a day of fishing on Cape Cod during their fresh-man year at Northeastern.

Reggie shoots over Derrick Battle during a game against East Carolina in January 1984.

Reggie dunks against Suffolk in December 1984.

Taking a break during a Celtics practice.

Reggie on the run in a February 1991 game.

Reggie slips between Billy Thompson and Kevin Edwards of the Miami Heat as Celtics Coach Jimmy Rodgers looks on.

Reggie's mother, Peggy, and sister, Sheron, look on as he signs autographs.

Reggie with his mother, Peggy, and father, Butch.

Reggie goes airborne against Cleveland.

The 1992 NBA All-Star Game.

Reggie leads a passing drill at the UMass/Boston Reggie Lewis Basketball Camp in 1992.

Fielding questions and dispensing advice, Reggie speaks to children at a UMass/Boston basketball camp.

Reggie tries his hand at hockey, without the skates, during a summer camp for kids at UMass/Boston.

A future star gets some expert guidance at the 1992 Reggie Lewis Camp at UMass/Boston.

Reggie and Reggie, Jr. at the 1993 Celtics rookie camp.

Reggie burns the Heat with his patented pull-up jumper.

Reggie is dazed after collapsing during a playoff game against the Charlotte Hornets on April 29, 1993.

Reggie and his wife Donna listen to Dr. Gilbert Mudge's optimistic diagnosis at a May 1993 news conference at Brigham & Women's Hospital in Boston.

Thousands turn out to honor Reggie on the day of his funeral in Boston.

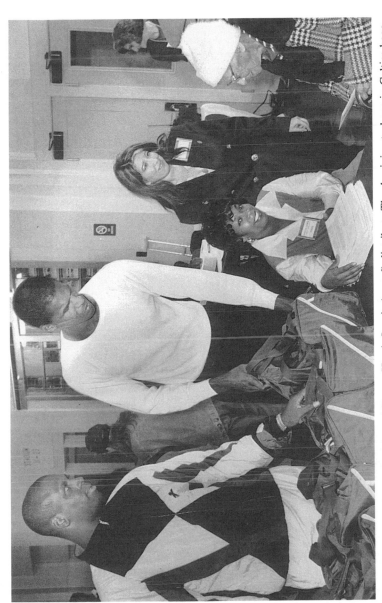

Xavier McDaniel, Robert Parish, and Donna Harris Lewis (seated) distribute Thanksgiving turkeys in Celtics bags at the annual Reggie Lewis Turkey Giveaway at Northeastern University in November 1993.

Joe Dickens and his son, Joe, Jr., Reggie's oldest nephew, wearing a jersey given to him by his uncle.

Reggie's mother, Peggy, at the basketball court where he first played the game, Collington Square in Baltimore. Reggie's footprints appear in the cement in front of her.

PHOTO CREDITS

The photographs appearing in this section have been used with the permission of their respective copyright owners, and their kindness is very much appreciated. The owners of these photographs, identified by page number, are as follows:

156 Photo Options
157 Inez Ritch
158 Photo Options
159 Inez Ritch

160 Photo Options
161 Inez Ritch
162 Photo Options
163 Robert Wade

164 Inez Ritch
165 Inez Ritch
166 Mark Reeves
167 Jim Wilson / Boston Globe

168 Michael Quan / Boston Globe
169 Bill Greene / Boston Globe
170 John Blanding / Boston Globe
171 Tom Herde / Boston Globe

172 Inez Ritch
173 Inez Ritch
174 Bill Brett / Boston Globe
175 Andrew Bernstein/NBA Photos

176 UMass/Boston Athletic Dept.
177 UMass/Boston Athletic Dept.
178 UMass/Boston Athletic Dept.
179 UMass/Boston Athletic Dept.

180 Barry Chas / Boston Globe
181 Pam Berry / Boston Globe
182 Bill Brett / Boston Globe
183 Frank O'Brien / Boston Globe

184 Yunghi Kim / Boston Globe
185 Lane Turner / Boston Globe
186 Photo Options
187 Photo Options

Career Statistics

NORTHEASTERN UNIVERSITY

Year	Games Played	Field Goal Percentage	Free Throw Percentage	Rebounds Per Game	Assists Per Game	Points Per Game
1983-84	32	.528	.688	6.2	1.5	17.8
1984-85	31	.503	.746	7.8	1.8	24.1
1985-86	30	.474	.803	9.3	2.2	23.8
1986-87	29	.489	.761	8.5	1.5	23.3
Totals	**122**	**.497**	**.756**	**7.9**	**1.7**	**22.2**

BOSTON CELTICS

Year	Games Played	Field Goal Percentage	Free Throw Percentage	Rebounds Per Game	Assists Per Game	Points Per Game
Regular Season						
1987-88	49	.466	.702	1.3	0.5	4.5
1988-89	81	.486	.787	4.7	2.7	18.5
1989-90	79	.496	.808	4.4	2.8	17.0
1990-91	79	.491	.826	5.2	2.5	18.7
1991-92	82	.503	.851	4.8	2.3	20.8
1992-93	80	.470	.867	4.3	3.7	20.8
Totals	**450**	**.488**	**.824**	**4.3**	**2.6**	**17.6**
Playoffs						
1987-88	12	.382	.600	1.3	0.3	2.4
1988-89	3	.473	.692	7.0	3.7	20.3
1989-90	5	.597	.771	5.0	4.4	20.2
1990-91	11	.487	.824	6.2	2.9	22.4
1991-92	10	.528	.762	4.3	3.9	28.0
1992-93	1	.636	.750	2.0	3.0	17.0
Totals	**42**	**.510**	**.777**	**4.2**	**2.6**	**17.5**

Index

Adenovirus type 2 151
Ainge, Danny 96
Aloha Classic 87
Annual Turkey Giveaway
    103, 104, 111
Aorta 153
Atlantic Coast Conference
    87
Auerbach, Red 92
Aunt Cookie 5, 9, 11, 33,
    34, 129
Aunt Dot 6, 52
Aunt Harriet 6
Autopsy 151-153

Baltimore City Hospital 5
Baltimore City Public
    Schools Championship
    48, 58
Baltimore Neighborhood
    Basketball League (BNBL)
    29, 40
Baseball 3, 15

Basketball Weekly 55
Bias, Len 67
Bicycles 14, 94
Bird, Larry 96-101, 117,
    118, 122
Bogues, Tyrone "Muggsy"
    28, 40-43, 51, 54, 55, 58,
    87, 93, 119
Boston Celtics 71, 85,
    92-96, 101, 102, 117-124,
    141, 154
Boston College 73
Boston Garden 71, 93, 110,
    115, 120, 154
Boston Globe 84, 153
Boston Herald 152
Boston, Massachusetts
    56, 65
Boyd, Damon 3
Boys and Girls Clubs of
    Boston 116
Brandeis University 130
Bridgeport, Connecticut 77